The Commonsense Book of Wine

The Commonsense Book of Wine

By

LEON D. ADAMS

REVISED EDITION

Foreword by

DR. MAYNARD A. AMERINE

DAVID McKAY COMPANY, INC.
NEW YORK

Library of Congress Catalog Card Number 58-12256

MANUFACTURED IN THE UNITED STATES OF AMERICA

Revised Edition 1964
Reprinted August 1971

To Eleanor

FOREWORD

MR. ADAMS IS uniquely qualified to write this book. He is the former public-relations expert for the California wine industry, a private wine consultant, a lover of wines of all kinds, and no mean protagonist for them. As the former secretary of the Wine Institute, he has had the unique opportunity of observing the highly competitive American wine market from all sides for a quarter of a century. His conclusions are provocative and stimulating.

For all who are devoted to California wines this book is most welcome. Here it is clearly and forcefully stated that wines should be measured on their own merits, not on outmoded historical or "fashionable" standards. This approach is all the more necessary since California wines have not been accorded their rightful place by many "experts"—experts who are often rather snobbish.

Standards there are indeed. But before standards can be applied, experience, training, and contemplation are necessary. The concern of this book is that the standards must be based on adequate consideration of these three primary requisites. Rightly, the emphasis is that quite unessential (or even misleading) standards are often employed in judging wine and that they should be avoided like the plague.

What a relief from the purists, who preach a sterile religion of vintages, châteaux, estate bottlings, and so on! Not that these are not important within a context of experience, training, and contemplation. The aesthetic differentiation of Chesapeake Bay oysters and Olympia oysters occurs only *after* we find that we can really differentiate them. This differentiation cannot occur until we are thoroughly familiar with both. The same is true with wines.

The author's point is that appreciation can start at any level, but that differentiation or ranking follows knowledge and understanding. His slightly ironic comments on the fallacy of ranking based on less than this experience are certainly justified. On the other hand, it is worth pointing out that ranking based on inexperienced "experts" is also meaningless. The text is devoted to inducing those who lack experience to acquire it forthwith.

It is clearly emphasized here that wines are more, much more, than alcohol. How much more they are than this depends on the approach of the consumer. Mr. Adams has set out the guideposts clearly for the beginner. If they lead to a greater use of wine, this book will fulfill the author's fondest hopes. If they also lead to a greater appreciation of wines, they will have made a noble contribution to finer and more sensible living in this country.

Bon appétit and prosit,
MAYNARD A. AMERINE

AUTHOR'S NOTE

THIS BOOK IS AN ATTEMPT to supply some common sense on a subject that needs it rather badly in this country. How badly is apparent from the thousands of questions Americans continually ask about wines, to which they are unable to obtain understandable answers. It is more glaringly apparent in millions of homes, restaurants, stores, and also, unfortunately, in our legislatures as well, where most of what is "known" about wine is simply not so. Even our national Congress, which prohibits the sale of Champagne in the District of Columbia on Sundays (but doesn't stop the flow of "sparkling white wine," which is the same thing), surely could stand considerable in the way of vinous enlightenment.

In an effort to answer the oftenest-asked wine questions, I have disclosed a few well-kept secrets and departed somewhat from orthodox viewpoints and style. To mention one minor example of the latter, academic purists will pardon me, I hope, for uniformly capitalizing the names of all wine types in the text. Also, because most

American vintners anglicize "Sauternes" by omitting the final "s" (presumably to negate any impression of plural meaning), I have done the same in referring to American Sauterne.

Hundreds of vintners and dozens of researchers, scholars, and authors in many lands have supplied the information contained here; I have only distilled the apparent facts from conflicting versions and have performed the condensation.

No vintner has read the manuscript; if some of them had, they might have caught errors it must inevitably contain. I know of no one of them who would be likely to agree with all of my views or with my statements of fact. This is not entirely surprising, for nobody—surely not the present author—knows all about wine.

I am deeply grateful to Dr. Maynard A. Amerine, the chairman of the Department of Viticulture and Enology of the University of California, whose global knowledge of wines has aided me in preparing the classification of wine flavors, colors, and alcoholic contents which follows the third chapter. Dr. Salvatore Pablo Lucia has been kind enough to review my several references to the health values of the product. And I also thank the few of my neighbors who have reviewed the text for clarity, making many valuable suggestions.

LEON D. ADAMS

CONTENTS

The Commonsense Book of Wine

CHAPTER 1

HOW TO BE A WINE SNOB

If you would enjoy fame as a wine expert, there is an easy way to acquire that reputation.

Next time you are served a glass of wine, lift it by the stem (not the bowl!). Wave it under your nose with a circular motion. Smell the wine, and look thoughtful. Take a sip, cautiously. Then, find fault with it. This is the sure-fire way to have others regard you as a connoisseur. Although it will get you by (it always works when I use it), you will only have qualified, thus far, as a wine snob.

If, on the other hand, you genuinely wish to cure your awe of unpronounceable wine labels, to hold your own in a wine discussion, to avoid being fleeced by nasty waiters, and to enjoy this delightful beverage without the risk of committing social hara-kiri, take heart now. These pages should unravel for you most of the mystery that enshrouds the thousands of different liquids known as wine.

Not the lack of information, but too much—information that baffles and bewilders those who seek simple guidance to gustatory pleasure—is largely responsible for this mystery. Millions of words are written and spoken in praise and explanation of wine without an explanation of the explanations. Meanwhile the product itself becomes increasingly entangled in a maze of overlapping type names, geographical designations, vintages, and general mumbo jumbo so confusing that it is quite unintelligible to ninety-nine out of a hundred storekeepers and restaurateurs who sell the product.

And the average American, who sometimes vaguely wonders what this or that bottle's contents might taste like, but who is not inclined to undertake lengthy investigations, usually just walks past the store shelf, or puts aside the restaurant's wine list, and buys beer, coke, or Bourbon instead.

Why does this hodgepodge continue to exist? Why don't wine labels tell in plain English what they mean? Who draws up those fearsome charts of vintage years and service temperatures, for what reason? Who decrees white wine with fish, red wine with red meat, long-stemmed glasses for Rhine, short ones for Burgundy? Why aren't the different kinds of wine given simple names, like those on the different kinds of canned soup, so that a novice can read the label and choose the vintage to serve with his meat balls?

Much of wine's complexity can be blamed on its charm. Its romantic qualities, possessed by no other food or drink, receive so much attention that they tend to obscure its simple function as a beverage.

The homage paid to wine is richly deserved. As the blood of the grape, bestowed by Nature with the magic power to create happiness, it has sacred religious symbolism. Its beginnings are lost in antiquity; its ancient history is traced from the hieroglyphics of Egypt and Babylon, from the writings of Greek and Roman poets and from no less than one hundred and sixty-five references in the Bible. Philosophers and physicians have sung wine's praises since the dawn of civilization, as an adjunct to life, health, and happiness. Modern gourmets and authors of cookbooks praise it as an inseparable companion of fine foods. Through all the ages of man it has been associated with feasting, philosophy, art, music, and love. Little wonder that its advocates strive to preserve these intangible, romantic qualities. It is also understandable that wine's proud heritage of tradition, although a source of much puzzlement to the general public, still largely governs its production and nomenclature.

Helping to weave the web more thickly are wine's stanchest friends and admirers, the connoisseur cult of Britain and America, whose number grows with the sales of gourmet books and with the worldwide expansion of such organizations as the international Wine and Food Society. These worshipers of Bacchus regard wine in the way the philatelist, who never uses his specimens to mail his letters, regards the stamps he collects. As they sip the object of their hobby (a kind of pleasure denied the stamp collectors), the wine fanciers discuss the optimum bottle age for Cabernet Sauvignon, the grievous error of serving *brut* Champagne with dessert, and fine distinctions between vintages—differences quite imperceptible to an average consumer and often also imperceptible (unless they peek at the labels) to the connoisseurs themselves.

Another wellspring of confusion is wine literature. Many excellent wine books are currently available to lay readers. Most of them praise the vintages of individual regions, debate wine's subtle food harmonies, or relate pleasant sojourns among the vineyards enjoyed by the authors. Although always delectable reading, they rarely spare space to rehearse the ABC's of wine. When an occasional writer does discuss the subject in grade-school terms, he leaps so abruptly to the post-graduate level that the novices among his readers are left completely befogged. Wine volumes heretofore published have thereby helped to create the need for the present one.

From the various sources I have mentioned, largely from gourmets and writers in Great Britain, but also in recent years from those of the United States, have also come many of the rules which surround fashionable wine selection and service. These rules did not come from the wine countries of Europe, where the average citizen consumes his wine as freely as most Americans gulp their ice water. The ordinary Frenchman, Italian, Spaniard, or Portuguese, to whom wine is among the staple necessities of life, is happily ignorant of its abracadabra, and if he ever were told that red wine should not be served with fish, would regard it as so much balderdash. (The Wine and Food Society has no chapters in continental Europe.)

American winegrowers have done little to clear up the maze. Most of them would be happier if their product could be freed of the enigmas and paradoxes which hinder its broader sale. Yet few would be willing to strip wine of its noble traditions and its undeniably valuable romantic atmosphere. Half-hearted attempts have occasionally been made to depart from the time-honored, but ambiguous, wine-type nomenclature inherited from Europe, only to be frustrated because the Old World wine names have become permanently anchored in the English language. And European vintners, whose principal customers already know how to buy and enjoy their merchandise, lack any motive to change their perplexing labels.

All of this confusion helps to make wine more intriguing than if it were simple. It also helps to account for the growing numbers of wine snobs. For on a subject as tangled as wine, almost anybody can expound safely, because hardly anyone else knows what is right or wrong.

What is wine snobbery? Let me first get my terms straight by distinguishing among wine experts, wine connoisseurs, and wine snobs.

A genuine wine expert is one who can readily distinguish among the world's principal wines without reading the labels. The number of such people is surprisingly few. You can become one, if your senses of taste and smell are keen, by sampling a sufficient number of wines with an open mind and a retentive memory, and by learning, at the same time, about the principal wine grape varieties and how wines are made.

To be a wine connoisseur, it is not necessary to be such an expert. Surely you are already a connoisseur (that is to say, a critical judge) of steaks, roasts, coffee, catsup, and also, perhaps, of Bourbon and cigarettes. In fact, we are all connoisseurs of the things we especially enjoy in food, drink, and entertainment. We are not shy about discussing our likes and dislikes among such items. Why be suddenly shy about our likes and dislikes among wines? Your taste is unique just as your thumb print is. You alone are the judge of what pleases your discriminating palate. I maintain that you are a connoisseur of wines when you have sampled enough of them to know which ones please you and which do not. My children, incidentally, were connoisseurs of wine by the time they were twelve years of age.

You are a wine snob, on the other hand, if (a) you look for a wine's faults instead of its virtues, if (b) you behave like an expert when you are not, if (c) you are influenced by a wine's price instead of by its flavor, if (d) you turn up your nose at bottles that lack famous names or vintage dates, if (e) you belittle wines simply because they do not come from Europe, or, in general, if you drink the label instead of the wine.

From the above distinctions it is readily apparent that while wine snobs are not necessarily experts or connoisseurs, you are likely to find many connoisseurs and some experts behaving like wine snobs.

Yet there is no particular harm in wine snobbery. In fact, it is fun, and might even be recommended as an easily acquired mark of gentility. Other cultural endeavors get welcome support from art snobs, book snobs, and music snobs, to name a few kinds. All of them enjoy themselves and derive benefit therefrom.

And since it is better to confess than to be exposed, I shall admit that in serving and discussing wines I occasionally practice a little snobbery myself.

Regardless, however, of whether you choose to become a wine snob, a connoisseur, or even a genuine wine expert, these pages, and especially the chapters on "Wine Unraveled," "Wine Shopper's Secrets," "Kinds for Every Use," and "Some Labels Unriddled," are likely to help you on your way.

CHAPTER 2

WHY DRINK IT?

IF A VINTNER WERE TO tell you, in one of his advertisements, that you ought to drink wine because it is the best of all tranquilizers—one product of nature that relaxes you gently with no harm to your system—he would be promptly taken to task by the United States Government, which has the power to revoke his license and put him out of business. There is a certain federal regulation, ambiguous in its language but backed up by some unambiguous bureaucratic rulings, that effectively prevents him from advertising this important truth.

Since it is high time that someone came forth with that best of all reasons (there are plenty of others!) why tension-tormented America should include wine in its daily diet, I may as well be the one, because I am not a vintner and therefore hold no license for the Government to revoke.

Before anyone asks "Aren't beer, whisky and gin the same as wine?" and "Are you advocating that we all become alcoholics?" let me answer both questions.

Wine is essentially a natural product; malt and distilled

beverages are manufactured. The grape is the only fruit that will preserve itself naturally, without anything being added or taken away. This is because it contains fermentable sugars and because the dustlike "bloom" on its skin contains natural yeasts that can ferment those sugars into alcohol. If we crush a handful of grapes and leave the juice in a cup, it will turn into wine.

There is a great deal more in wine than mere alcohol. It has been medically substantiated that wines, depending on their type, contain not only fruit sugars valuable in the human diet, but in addition are the only common alcoholic beverages containing significant quantities of the B vitamins, plus all of the thirteen mineral elements recognized as essential to maintain animal and human life. They also have the ability to improve appetite and promote digestion.

It is their non-alcoholic components, not found in spirituous beverages, that make wines behave differently in the human body. Somehow, in ways not yet fully understood by medical researchers, the organic acids, esters, and nitrogen-bearing compounds in wines *slow down* the rate at which the alcohol in wines enters your blood stream. The slow rate of absorption is important. Your blood-alcohol level, when you drink wine, reaches a plateau instead of a peak; the alcohol circulates at low levels through your body, where it lulls and helps to relax your jumpy nerve centers; you feel a pleasant glow. The pleasant feeling from wine lasts longer than that from other drinks. Alcohol from the others gets into your blood more quickly; its effects are more sudden and more pronounced.

In other words, don't drink wine for a "kick," because if it's a kick you want, you will get it fastest and hardest from vodka. Wine's alcoholic effect is more gradual.

If you haven't already discovered for yourself the relaxing quality of wine, ask a few of your friends if wine doesn't make them sleepy more readily than a stronger drink does. Or if you prefer the testimony of folklore, there's the jingle that goes:

"Candy's dandy
Wine's fine
But likker's quicker."

Some noted medical authorities have said that wine could well supplant 90 per cent of the drugs used to induce sleep. There is also reason to wonder whether Americans would be gulping 65,000,000 aspirin tablets every twenty-four hours to reduce pain (this was the rate calculated in 1957) if more people used wine.

Returning to the subject of tranquilizing drugs, pharmaceutical firms in France are unhappy because they cannot find many customers for their Miltowns and other happy-pills in that country, where nearly everyone drinks wine instead of water.

There is plentiful medical testimony that tension, stress, or chronic anxiety is a national disease among American adults in this age of nuclear bombs and sputniks. I suspect that if a survey were made among people who regularly have wine with dinner or who take a glass of Sherry before dinner, it would show that most of them enjoy emotional comfort in the evenings, sleep well, and need no manufactured tranquilizers. As one busy mother expressed it succinctly when I interviewed her in the course of a survey which I once conducted among Sherry consumers, "A glass of Sherry before dinner gets me past the suicide hour."

But since everyone knows that wine has been the joy of mankind for centuries, you may ask, at this point, how this beverage can make you happy when it also makes you drowsy. The answer is that it depends on the quantity consumed, the circumstances, and on your individual body chemistry at the time you drink wine. Some of us become happy, then sleepy. Others are relaxed at first, then joyful. Some stay wide-awake all evening.

Enough, however, about the tranquilizing, joy-promoting, and soporific qualities of wine, because in the chapter entitled "Is Wine for You?" I devote several pages to a number of surprising things doctors now know about how various alcoholic beverages behave when they get past your lips.

As for wine's appetite- and digestion-promoting values, these too are verboten in vintners' advertising. The Government even considers it a crime for a winery to quote the Bible passage in which Paul admonishes Timothy to "use a little wine for thy stomach's sake and thine often infirmities. . . ."

Note that Paul advises "a little" wine. Too much wine,

like too much whisky, too much medicine, too much salt, or even too much water, can injure or even kill.

Despite these taboos against circulating information that would cause wine consumption to skyrocket in America, other attractive—although less compelling—qualities of the product have caused its use to gain steadily.

As appreciation of good cooking spreads in America, wine's flavor magic as an accompaniment to tasty food is gradually winning this beverage a place on the better dinner tables of the nation. Thus far, however, this is occurring only in certain favored localities. You find wine always served where there is fine food; you never find it in homes or restaurants where hurried, tasteless meals are had with ice water as the beverage.

Vast areas of the United States and Canada have not as yet been subjected to the civilizing influence of flavorful cuisine. Most of the midwestern, southern, and northern states have not yet had their tastes refined by leisurely gourmet dining and its inseparable companion, wine. In those gastronomic deserts of America, wine, which enhances food flavors, cannot compete with catsup, which hides flavors that usually deserve to be hidden.

Yet there is hope for the future of gastronomy on this continent, because increasing travel to the oases of San Francisco, New York, New Orleans, and the wine countries of Europe is exposing millions of Americans to the delights of civilized dining. Also, increasing leisure always starts people searching for luxuries to make life richer. In this process wine inevitably wins acceptance.

There are powerful reasons for this. It is a fact, evident to anyone who gives it a moment's thought, that among all the common beverages of mankind, there is only one that is exclusively a mealtime beverage, made and used only for that single purpose. That description fits most of the world's wine—the class known as dry table wine.

The fermented juice of grapes is the only beverage that offers a complete range of the four taste elements to which the human palate is sensitive—sweetness, acidity, saltiness, and bitterness—to balance these same flavor elements in solid foods. In addition, wine supplies aroma, acidity, and smoothness to those foods lacking those qualities.

At the table, wine is a liquid to accompany solid food. Although used as a beverage, it also fulfills the function of a sauce, by accenting flavors of foods. With its additional values of supplying relaxation and a feeling of well-being, there is little wonder that, to most of its consumers throughout the world, wine is a regular part of the daily diet.

Aside from these weighty reasons for actually drinking the product, wine is also a glamorous ornament, a symbol of gracious living and of hospitality. No one item available to the dinner host or hostess can add as much charm to dining as wineglasses and a bottle on the table with the silver, china, and flowers—whether the guests drink it or not. Can you think of any other one thing that can perform this function as well?

Wine is also a handy conversation piece. Add its ability to keep the guests longer at the table, savoring the dishes whose flavors the wine improves, and you understand why the world's great chefs and gourmets insist that wine accompany their fine meals.

To celebrate an occasion or simply to make whoopee, some of us prefer to do so nicely. We cringe at broken furniture, at guests who have to be driven home, and similar unpleasantness. While wines can be imbibed too freely and sometimes are, the earlier described differences in effects of different alcoholic beverages are reasons why some of us choose to serve the more temperate beverage as our social lubricant.

For temperate it is, by comparison with the other forms of alcohol. Not in alcoholic content, because a highball usually contains no more alcohol than the average diner's intake of dinner wine; but for the reasons earlier mentioned, plus the fact that most wine is consumed with food, which absorbs much of the alcohol and keeps it from entering the blood stream. Wine simply does not overstimulate.

You have observed many Americans, Britons, and individuals of other non-wine-using groups, in various stages of intoxication. But how many wine-drinking Frenchmen and Italians have you ever seen tottering from drunkenness? In my own travels in the wine countries of Europe, I have yet to see anyone, except visitors from the non-wine-using nations, intoxicated in public.

The testimony of police and probation officers in the United States is that alcohol figures importantly in the juvenile misbehavior that has plagued this country increasingly since World War II. Brooklyn's Judge Samuel S. Leibowitz, following a visit to Italy, expressed his amazement at the low percentage of juvenile crime in that country, and credited it to the fact that, in Italy, fathers are still the heads of their households. He might as readily have noted that in Italy children are reared in wine-drinking homes and are given wine, diluted with water, from babyhood. This, incidentally, has also been the case in my own family, which has not yet produced one case of alcoholism.

So much for youth, whose behavior this beverage might help to improve; but for the old, wine becomes well nigh a necessity. Dr. Salvatore P. Lucia, in *Wine as Food and Medicine,* expresses it as follows:

> Wine, the handmaiden for those myriad social and festive functions of a vigorous and youthful life, becomes a balm for the convalescent and "milk" for the aged. The autumnal years of life, usually burdened by disenchantment and fatigue, and often lament, become bearable behind the aura of a glass of pleasant wine.... Whether wine be considered as sedative, medicine, food, digestive aid, or a factor in longevity, it is indisputably a boon to the aged.

With all these recommendations, the blood of the grape also represents economy. In most parts of the United States, despite a burden of taxes greater than the cost of the product itself, it is the best bargain the public can buy in a beverage with alcoholic content. In most of America, a bottle of wine could still be purchased, during 1964, for little more than a dollar, and in some states for considerably less.

Why drink wine? Ernest Hemingway may have answered that question best when he wrote:

> Wine is one of the most civilized things in the world and one of the natural things of the world that has been brought to the greatest perfection; and it offers a greater range for enjoyment and appreciation than possibly any other purely sensory thing which may be purchased.

CHAPTER 3

WINE UNRAVELED

IN A BOSTON RESTAURANT noted for its delectable lobster dishes I ordered "a dry white dinner wine—any kind you happen to have." The waitress nodded knowingly, and brought me a bottle of White Port.

In a San Francisco store a matron asked for Château d'Yquem. When the clerk moved to the cheese counter and began fumbling among packages, the customer added: "It's a wine I want."

"Why didden you say so?" he demanded, and handed her a bottle of Muscatel.

Such incidents, of which I can recite dozens, evoke no smiles, but only groans, from vintners. They are especially distressing to me, because I once undertook the Augean project of directing the education of Americans in the understanding and appreciation of wine. And because I felt that any product, in order to achieve general use, must first have clear identity, much of my labor during twenty years in the Wine Institute was aimed at making sense out of wine nomenclature.

The latter effort even led me some years ago to write a correspondence course on the subject. It was called the Wine Study Course, and was based upon four booklets which I entitled the *Wine Handbook Series.* In the *Handbooks* I slashed through all of the world's wine lists, and arbitrarily reduced the thousands of kinds of wine to only five classes. (The classifications I chose were: "Appetizer," "White Table," "Red Table," "Dessert," and "Sparkling." These subsequently achieved legal status in government regulations.) This, I imagined at the time, was simple enough to make sense to anyone.

More than half a million *Handbooks* were printed. Over a period of years a quarter million people signed up for the Study Course. Some fifty thousand, in thirty-four countries around the globe, studied the books, passed written examinations, and received Certificates of Merit as graduates. The wine industry's advertisements, publicity releases, booklets, and leaflets by millions and billions saturated the nation, repeating the *Handbooks'* simplification of wine.

Yet in most of the United States the kind of confusion about wine names which the Boston and San Francisco cases illustrate continues to exist—among tradesfolk, among consumers, and even, to a considerable extent, among the very people who produce and import wines.

What harm is there in the confusion? Plenty. It is one of the principal factors that prevent wine—the beverage of civilized dining and true temperance—from attaining wide use in the United States. Millions of Americans have tasted wine and spat it out as disagreeable, simply because they have tried the wrong kinds. They say: "I don't like wine," because the types they have tasted are the ones with dry, tart, astringent flavors that only become pleasing with long-repeated use by the individual. Meanwhile, hundreds of other wines, with tastes virtually any beginner would like at the very first sip, are hidden behind names that are meaningless to the uninitiated buyer. The labels of most wines tell nothing of their flavors.

But won't this situation straighten itself out eventually?

No, it will not. To the contrary, it becomes increasingly tangled each year, especially as the volume of imports from Europe increases and adds to the number of mysterious names you see on wine stores' shelves. This book, therefore, includes a new effort to unscramble the vinous crazy quilt.

It attempts to tell you, in so far as possible, what a wine's label rarely tells: how that particular wine is likely to taste if you open the bottle and pour yourself a glassful. You will find that information in the pages entitled "Wine Flavors, Colors, and Alcoholic Contents" at the end of this chapter.

I emphasize *in so far as possible* for several reasons, one of which is that nobody to my knowledge has ever assembled such a wine classification in printed form before. Another reason is that—as you will see in my lists—many single wine names are used to represent two or more different-colored, different-tasting wines. (This naturally confounds the buyer, but the vintners—because *they* know what they intend their names to mean—see nothing at all wrong with the practice.)

Still another is that most of our winegrowing friends keep changing the sweetness and acidity of their wines from year to year—a form of vintner's license that contributes to the everlasting bafflement of their customers. Some individual wines even slip completely out of their normal flavor categories from time to time, without any warning to the people who buy them.

Many of the wines bearing different names cannot be told apart by experts without seeing their labels. This is one of the things that provide our wine snobs with opportunities to display their knowledge.

It is probably a form of Bacchic blasphemy to treat wine, the most honored of all beverages, as merely another drink. Yet soda pop—in contrast to the blood of the grape—comes in only about twenty most popular flavors. Beer has four, more or less; whisky, perhaps six; and the dairy industry now offers us, as beverages, homogenized milk, condensed, evaporated, and powdered milks, buttermilk, skim milk, chocolate milk, and for folks with certain allergies, goat's milk. Why not group wines, too, according to their principal flavors?

To this question vintners usually reply that the products of the world's myriad vineyards cannot be classified as simply as the manufactured uniform flavors of soft drinks. They point out that wines are farm products, as temperamental as the local weather that influences the flavors of their grapes, just as it influences the taste of apples, plums, peaches, and other fruits and vegetables from season to season. This is why most wines are named for places, some for the specific localities where they are grown, and others for the districts where their types originated centuries ago. Other wines display names of the rare, sometimes unpronounceable grape varieties from which they are made, but this, too, involves geography, because the same variety grown in two different localities may produce two quite different wines.

Although there are a few world-traveled experts who know the local geography of many grape-growing regions, and who even possess some knowledge of grape ampelography, the combination of such wine names—to the average American—is merely euphonious gibberish. My lists serve to illustrate the name jumble that faces any shopper who might want to taste a wine's flavor—not its label.

Nevertheless, my flavor groupings at least give you a preliminary idea of how a given wine is likely to taste if you happen to buy it. I will even go a step farther and venture that if you have already found that you enjoy any *one* of the wines listed in only a single group, there is a reasonable possibility that you also will like most of the others with which I have classed it.

Some readers may also find a partial answer to the question often asked by those who return from trips abroad: "Where can I find an American wine like the one I enjoyed in Europe?" The Meursault you liked in France is grouped with its California relatives, Chardonnay and

Pinot Blanc. If Red Bordeaux pleased you, so will any well-made Cabernet; and so on.

Vintners may approve some of my descriptions, but may protest the helter-skelter way in which I have arbitrarily tossed their favorite products into broad flavor categories with neighbors they regard as common. They will surely disagree with me on certain points. For that matter, vintners do not agree on these things among themselves. Let me illustrate with one bit of history.

Some years ago the staff of the Wine Institute, appalled by the confusion then existing, undertook to prepare a set of definitions of the principal California wine types and to write them into a state regulation to guide producers, merchants, and beverage-control officials. The importance of the undertaking can be appreciated when one remembers that California supplies more than three fourths of all wine consumed in the United States.

Our staff research into European laws and regulations cast no light. In Europe, we found, elaborate laws mainly define the many hundreds of little viticultural regions and limit vineyard and winery practices, but fail to specify how a wine under a given name shall taste.

We then quizzed California vintners, individually and at industry meetings, on what their labels meant. We soon learned that one winery's Sauterne matched another winery's Haut Sauterne; that John Doe's Sherry was drier than Richard Roe's "Dry" Sherry; and so on through the entire list of popular types.

Using more wheedling than logic, we finally won most

leading wineries' agreement to let us spell out measurable steps of sweetness for "dry," "regular," "haut" (sweet), and "château" (still sweeter) Sauternes, and for "dry," "regular," and "cream" (sweet, "golden," or "mellow") Sherries.

The day arrived for the official state of California hearing on the proposed regulations. Before the time came to discuss Sauterne, the spokesman for a group of wineries made an announcement. "We are artists," he said. "We cannot agree to make our wines all the same. We oppose any definition for Sauternes."

Unable to answer that one, we contented ourselves with establishing the definitions of the three not-too-rigid sweetness levels for Sherries, which scraped through the hearing with only minor opposition.

If you ever have occasion to read the California regulations—which I am not recommending for entertainment—please remember that, confusing though they are, no other wine regulations in the world give nearly as much flavor information as these do.

It is unfortunate that Italian, Spanish, and Portuguese wines do not display—as most French and German labels do nowadays—the partially informative legends you read in small type, such as "Red Bordeaux Wine," "White Burgundy Wine," "Semi-dry White Vouvray Wine," and "Rhine Wine." These represent at least one tiny step toward giving the public a hint of a wine's color and flavor. For if there ever was a product that required lucid descriptions of taste on its labels—and also, for that matter, full "directions for use" on every bottle—that product is wine.

My new attempt at mapping the wine nomenclature forest covers only a limited area—*those names found oftenest on wine bottles in stores in the United States.* All of the names—United States and foreign—are thrown together in alphabetical arrangement with no attempt to group those that are synonymous or nearly so. The lists are admittedly skimpy, being limited to the tasting experience of a few friends and myself and checked against the available foggy literature.

Unfortunately, too, my grouping of principal names may not help you much in reading restaurant wine lists, because most such lists refer to foreign wines by their vineyard or village names—not even by their regional appellations.

My lists do not recommend any specific types for you, because each individual finds his personal choice among wines, as he does among friends, sweethearts, newspapers, magazines, music, or neckties. I have attempted here to unravel only the bare designations that imply flavors, color, and alcoholic strength. The strange meanings of some other words and symbols that you see displayed on wine bottles are explained in a later chapter entitled "Some Labels Unriddled."

WINE FLAVORS, COLORS, AND ALCOHOLIC CONTENTS

Grouped here are the wine names found oftenest on bottle labels in stores throughout the United States, according to their usual color, their approximate alcoholic strength, and their usual principal flavors. I lump them together regardless of their European or American origins.

At least half of these names represent two or more different-tasting or different-colored wines. Such names with multiple meanings are necessarily repeated under more than one heading, but I have marked them conveniently with asterisks (*).

Also, many of the names given are partly or wholly synonymous with others in the same alphabetical groups. Because you see them so often on bottles, I include words like Liebfraumilch and Gevrey-Chambertin, even though a careful inspection of their labels would usually disclose (in small type) additional legends reading "Rhine Wine" on the former and "Burgundy Red Wine" on the latter. Hundreds of European village names and many of the French district appellations of origin are omitted because they appear in the United States with less frequency.

Also omitted from the lists are the fruit wines—blackberry, loganberry, strawberry, currant, apple, pear wine (perry), and the rest—because their names clearly tell you their principal flavors. All of them, or nearly all, are very sweet, and most are in the alcoholic content range of 12 to 14 per cent. An exception is apple wine; most of the samples I have tasted are 20 per cent.

The groups headed "red" include wines ranging all the way from tawny to ruby. "White" means wines that are either straw-colored, golden, or light amber. The alcoholic-content figures only represent averages for the products most widely sold. Individual wines may vary a few degrees in strength.

"Dry" as used here means without sugar—the exact opposite of "sweet." This is not how the labels read, however, because most vintners —unwilling to label their wines "sweet" because they believe it impedes their sales—make them sweet but label them "dry."

By "slightly sweet" I mean the taste you get from one lump of sugar in your coffee. "Medium sweet" would represent a second or third lump, "sweet" a fourth or fifth. (I am describing sweet *taste,* not measuring sugar as wine chemists do, which is quite a different matter.)

"Astringent" means puckery, the same mouth sensation you get from overly strong tea. "Labrusca" refers to the grape flavor you get in most bottled and canned grape juice; it is the "foxy" personality of the Concord grape variety and its many relatives. ("Labrusca" is the viticulturist's name for this family of wild American vines.)

WHITE "TABLE" WINES

(Average Alcoholic Content 11 to 12 per cent)

Dry–Tart

Bordeaux Blanc *
Chablis
Chardonnay
Chassagne
Dry Sauterne
Dry Semillon
Emerald Riesling *
Folle Blanche
Graves *
Green Hungarian
Grey Riesling
Johannisberger Riesling *
Lacrima Christi *
Lafões
Meursault
Moselle *
Mountain White
Muscadet
Neuchatel
Niersteiner *
Orvieto
Piesporter *
Pinot Blanc
Pinot Chardonnay
Pouilly-Fuissé
Pouilly-sur-Loire
Puligny-Montrachet
Rhein *
Rheingau *
Rheinhessen *
Rheinpfalz *
Rhine Wine *
Rhine Wine (California)
Riesling *
Sauterne (California) *
Soave
Sylvaner *
Traminer *
Verdicchio
Vouvray *
White Bordeaux *
White Burgundy
White Chianti
White Pinot
White Riesling *

Dry–Labrusca Flavor

Rhine Wine (American, New York State, Ohio, et cetera) *
Delaware *
Niagara *

Completely dry wines are not ordinarily liked by beginners at very first taste. You get to like such wines after repeated use, the way you gradually acquire a taste for strong cheeses, green olives, or black, unsweetened coffee. Note, however, that many of the above names are marked (*) to show that they also appear in other flavor groups. You will find some of them in the groups of sweeter white wines.

WHITE "TABLE" WINES (Continued)

Dry to Sweet—Spicy Flavors

Dry Sauvignon Blanc
Gewürz Traminer
Light Dry Muscat
Light Muscat
Light Sweet Muscat
Malvasia Bianca
Sauvignon Blanc

California Gewürz Traminer is usually dry; the Alsatian version is frequently sweet. Some "Light Muscat" and Sauvignon Blanc wines are dry, others sweet.

Medium Sweet

Chenin Blanc
Emerald Riesling *
Graves *
Haut Sauterne *
Johannisberger Riesling *
Lacrima Christi *
Liebfraumilch
Moselle *
Niersteiner *
Piesporter *
Rhein *
Rheingau *
Rheinhessen *
Rheinpfalz *
Rhine Wine *
Riesling *
Sauterne *
Sylvaner *
Traminer *
Vouvray *
White Riesling *

Medium Sweet—Labrusca Flavor

Rhine Wine (American, New York, Ohio, et cetera) *
Delaware *
Niagara *

Sweet

Barsac
"Château" Sauterne
Chenin Blanc
Haut Sauterne *
Sauterne *
Sweet Sauvignon Blanc
Sweet Semillon
Vin Santo *

Herb-flavored—Sweet

May Wine (Woodruff flavor)

RED "TABLE" WINES

(Average Alcoholic Content 12 per cent)

Dry—Tart—Usually Astringent

Aloxe-Corton *	Claret	Pinot Noir
Barbaresco	Clos de Vougeot *	Pomerol
Barbera	Gamay *	Pommard *
Barberone	Gevrey-Chambertin *	Red Bordeaux
Barolo	Graves *	Red Pinot
Beaujolais	Grignolino *	Red Rhone Wine
Beaune *	Haut-Médoc	Rioja
Bordeaux Rouge	Hermitage	Saint-Émilion
Burgundy *	Mâcon *	Saint-Estèphe
Cabernet	Margaux	Saint-Julien
Cabernet Sauvignon	Médoc	Valpolicella
Charbono	Mountain Red	Volnay *
Châteauneuf-du-Pape	Nebbiolo	Vosne-Romanée *
Chianti (Red)	Nuits Saint-Georges *	Zinfandel

The warning to neophytes about how the completely dry white wines taste at first sip goes double with the dry, tart, astringent reds. You may possibly like them with spaghetti and similar Italian foods, but usually the really dry red wines require extended taste training. As with the whites, some of the above names are also used on slightly sweet wines; see below.

Slightly Sweet—Soft

Aloxe-Corton *	Clos de Vougeot *	"Vino"
Beaune *	Gevrey-Chambertin *	Volnay *
Burgundy *	Nuits Saint-Georges *	Vosne-Romanée *
Chambertin *	Pommard *	

"Vinos"—soft, sweetish California wines with Italian-sounding brand names—are readily liked by beginners, and require little taste training. But all the other wines listed above, except Volnay, also come dry and astringent.

Sweet—Mild Flavors

Miscellaneous proprietary brand names—some after famous women of history.

Very Sweet—Labrusca Flavor

Concord	"Kosher"	Malaga (American)

PINK "TABLE" WINES

(Average Alcoholic Content 12 per cent)

Dry–Tart

Gamay Rosé *
Grenache Rosé *
Grignolino *
Mâcon *
Rosé *
Tavel
Vin Rosé *

You almost never know whether a Rosé is going to be dry, sweet, or in-between, until you discover what each vintner means by his individual label. Most of those I have tasted under labels qualified by grape names such as Gamay and Grenache have happened to be quite dry. Some American producers use the word *vin* (French for "wine") to designate their dry pink wines from their sweet ones, or—to confuse things further—to do the opposite.

Medium Sweet to Sweet

Grenache Rosé *
Pink Wine *
Rosé *
Vin Rosé *

"APPETIZER" WINES

(Average Alcoholic Content 19 per cent)

Dry—Pale Gold or Light Amber—"Nutty"

Amontillado Sherry *
Bone Dry Sherry
Cocktail Sherry *
Dry Sherry *
Extra Dry Sherry
Fino Sherry
Madeira *
Manzanilla
Marsala *
Montilla *
Sherry *

"Nutty" refers to the characteristic oxidized or *rancio* flavor of Sherries, Madeiras, and Marsalas. The Spanish Finos and Montillas and a few of the California Sherries have a distinctly different kind of *rancio* taste, and are sometimes called *flor* Sherries; but that word rarely appears on a label.

Dry—Herb-Flavored

American White Vermouth
Dry Vermouth
French-type Vermouth
French Vermouth

Slightly Sweet—"Nutty"

Amontillado Sherry *
Cocktail Sherry *
Dry Sherry *
Madeira *
Marsala *
Montilla *
Oloroso Sherry *
Sherry *

Sweet—"Nutty"

Brown Sherry
Cream Sherry
Golden Sherry
Mellow Sherry
Madeira *
Marsala *
Oloroso Sherry *

Sweet—Herb-flavored

Italian Vermouth
Italian-type Vermouth
Sweet Vermouth

"APÉRITIF" WINES

(Alcoholic Content Usually About 20 per cent)

I can tell you that virtually all wines with "apéritif" on their labels are definitely sweet, that a few of them taste like the white sweet Vermouth that is a popular ladies' drink in Italy, that all of them are made to be served ice cold, and that they blend well with soda, ginger ale, tonic, and soft drinks. But beyond that my attempt to chart wine flavors seems to break down, because the additional flavors of these wines cover a vast range—from orange and lime to chocolate and coffee—and include the subtle tastes imparted by numerous herbs. (The spiced and herb-flavored wines of the ancients developed into modern Vermouths, which are also apéritif wines.) For many years the only apéritif wines that enjoyed any popularity in the United States were woodruff-flavored May wine and Dubonnet, a sweet red wine resembling Port but with an added distinctive flavor of its own. But after 1955, when the Government first authorized "special natural wines" to contain natural pure flavors, a flood of new products appeared on the American market with exotic coined names resembling nothing in the universe of wine—ranging from birds and animals to textiles and cars. By 1958 their acceptance appeared permanent, and most of the major American vintners, revising their old concepts of what constitutes wine, were working overtime concocting additional new flavors. This group of products offers new taste adventures among products of the grape.

WHITE "DESSERT" WINES

Sweet—Usual Alcoholic Content About 20 per cent

Angelica
White Port

Sweet—Usual Alcoholic Content About 16 per cent

Light White Port
Vin Santo *

Sweet—Muscat Flavor—Usually 20 per cent

Muscat Frontignan
Muscatel

PINK "DESSERT" WINES

Sweet—Usually 20 per cent

Tokay (California)
A number of specialty wines
with proprietary names

California Tokay is pink-amber and less sweet than Port.

RED "DESSERT" WINES

Sweet—About 20 per cent

Mavrodaphne
Port
Ruby Port
Tawny Port

The traditional Port and the Ruby are sometimes sweeter than the Tawny sub-type. "American," "New York State," and other eastern and midwestern states' Ports are likely to have some Labrusca flavor.

Sweet—Muscat Flavor—20 per cent

Aleatico
Black Muscat
Red Muscatel

Sweet—About 16 per cent

Light Port

SPARKLING WINES

(Average Alcoholic Content 12 per cent)

White—Dry

Champagne *Brut* *
Champagne *Nature*

White—Medium Sweet

Champagne *Brut* *
Extra Dry Champagne
Sparkling Lacrima Christi
Sparkling Moselle

White—Sweet

Champagne *Demi-Sec*
Champagne *Doux*
Champagne *Goût-Américain*
Champagne *Sec*
Dry Champagne

White—Sweet—Muscat Flavor

Asti Spumante
Sparkling Muscat

Pink—Dry

Pink Champagne *
Sparkling Rosé *

Pink—Medium Sweet

Crackling Rosé
Pink Champagne *
Sparkling Rosé *

Red—Medium Sweet

Champagne Rouge
Red Champagne
Sparkling Burgundy

Expect virtually all sparkling wines that are labeled "New York State" or "Ohio" (and some of those called "American") to have distinct Labrusca flavors. There are two other classes of effervescent wines occasionally found on the market. One consists of carbonated wines which, except for one pink Portuguese specialty, are seldom seen nowadays. The other group is called "crackling," *pétillant* or *frizzante*—terms which mean the wines sparkle only faintly. Most of these are white or pink.

CHAPTER 4

WINE SHOPPER'S SECRETS

THE MAJORITY OF WINE PRODUCERS and importers who chance to read this chapter are likely to disapprove of its blunt language. It is an earnest attempt to help you select wines that will fit your taste, purse, and purpose.

No industry, except perhaps the makers of photographic supplies, makes it harder for the uninformed consumer to buy its merchandise than the vintners do, with their flowery advertisements which exhort without informing, and their mysterious labels which few storekeepers and restaurateurs—let alone the puzzled public—can understand.

Thousands of people are continually asking those of us who are supposed to know: "What wine shall I buy?" Sometimes the questioner adds, with a note of despair: "Never mind giving me a lecture; just tell me the name of the wine and where I can get it." If I could answer the question simply, I would do so.

I can name for you, on the day this paragraph is written, a number of individual brands and types which are likely to please you, if you buy them right now in the San Francisco Bay area. By the time you read this my advice may be out of date; and it would not guide you safely, anyhow, in Pittsburgh, Bangor, Indianapolis, or even in Los Angeles. Some of the finest wines can be bought only in a few American cities.

Many other books have recommended lists of specific wines by brands and types. I am stating the reasons this book does not. Wines, unlike most other processed foods and beverages, are constantly changing, as the weather in the vineyards changes from season to season, almost the way apples and other fresh fruits do. Few vintners are able to continue putting into their bottles, month in and month out, exactly the same blends under each of their type labels. I doubt whether you can buy a duplicate of any wine in my own cellar. Certainly no store in your city can sell you the identical wine which won a gold medal in any of the recent annual quality competitions. Even the wine in an individual bottle continues aging and changing while it is being shipped and while it stands in the store; and, too often, it may even have spoiled before you buy it. Besides, wineries change hands, while the founding dates on their labels do not.

These are some of the reasons wines are always an interesting topic of conversation; they are, in fact, part of its charm. They are also reasons why the next few pages, which contain some secrets known to hardened wine shoppers, may make your wine buying easier.

If you are not now a wine buyer, and are about to get

your feet wet for the first time, it is pertinent to note that nobody ever learned to swim from a textbook. The only way to decide whether you will like or dislike rutabaga, endive, water cress, or other unfamiliar vegetables is to taste them. Likewise, to find which wine flavors please you, you have to taste enough of them.

Don't give up too easily, because it has been proved conclusively, by scientific taste tests administered to thousands of people, that somewhere in the wonderfully wide flavor spectrum of wines there are always one or more nectars to delight each individual's palate.

The best and least expensive way to sample different wines (and this is a handy method for experienced wine shoppers, too) is to visit one of the wineries which offer free tasting for their visitors. There are scores of such wineries in California, Ohio, and New York. You might also get yourself invited to one of the wine-tasting parties at which vintners supply free wines, which they do frequently in a number of American cities whose state laws permit it.

If you are not fortunate enough to live in or visit one of these favored localities, perhaps some kind friend will serve you a wine which you discover you like (in which case be sure to copy the label and learn exactly where he bought it). Otherwise you will have to pay your way in the tasting department.

Ordinarily, this means investing a few dollars in pure shopping adventure. It involves buying different types and brands more or less at random, taking them home and sampling them.

Why not invite a few friends to share the expense and the fun of a do-it-yourself wine tasting? Hide the labels, number the bottles, and keep score of the wines best liked. Then unveil the labels to identify your choices. The wines you don't happen to like can be given to someone else to whom their flavor is appealing.

If you don't tire in the process, you will eventually be rewarded. For, as that renowned wine judge, Dr. Charles Pierre Mathé, always says: "Wine is like American business. When it's good, it's very good; when it's bad, it's still pretty good!"

You may wonder, why not just ask the dealer to recommend a wine you will enjoy? This is a splendid idea and a convenient short cut, if, repeat if, you can find a merchant who regularly drinks and enjoys wine himself, and thereby knows what he is talking about. Don't just ask a clerk. He is likely to recommend either the wine that pays the store the widest profit margin, or one which the store is closing out; or, having never tasted any of the wines, he simply won't know what to suggest. Since dealers who know wines are lamentably scarce in most of these United States, you are probably left to explore on your own.

Let's focus on a single typical first-time shopping expedition, and assume that you contemplate buying a wine to serve with hors d'oeuvre or potato chips before dinner. This is an easy beginning, because most people, including even some store clerks, remember from movies or novels that one kind of wine often served before a meal is Sherry. But the average store shelf contains bottles labeled "Sherry," "Cream Sherry," "Dry Sherry," "Extra Dry Sherry," "Cocktail Sherry," and occasionally some called "Bone Dry Sherry." Which to buy?

A good idea is to purchase two or three different kinds —dry, cream, and just plain Sherry—a bottle (preferably a small one) of each. Take them home and give your guests a choice. Note carefully which one was best liked. At this point you will already be something of a Sherry connoisseur!

"Hold on!" you may protest. "Do I have to spend all that money?" The answer is: relax and buy freely, because wines are far and away the best beverage bargains in America. In the average store three small bottles of different Sherries can be had for less than half the price of a single fifth of bottled-in-bond Bourbon.

Giving your guests a choice of flavors is also advisable when you are shopping for table wines. Serving more than one kind of wine is always a good idea, because just as you may like your coffee unsweetened while your table neighbor dumps six lumps into his cup, our individual tastes vary sharply between dry and sweet wines.

Which table types to buy for a start? Try one small bottle each of Rosé, Sauterne, and Burgundy. Or if you prefer fancier names, select any flavor relatives of those three types as listed in the chapter entitled "Wine Unraveled."

In selecting table wines, however, the wise shopper—

just as he is careful not to buy over-soft tomatoes or a tired head of lettuce—also takes similar precautions with this class of wine. That is because table wines are perishable—almost as perishable, under some conditions, as milk. Especially avoid buying a bottle whose label has grown yellow and frayed from overlong storage in the store.

Here I recommend the philosophy of the wise housewife who went to her butcher and said: "I am having relatives in for dinner. How many chickens have you?"

The butcher counted: "Twelve."

"Pick out your eight toughest ones," she directed.

He did so with alacrity.

"I'll take the other four," she said.

The surest way to avoid getting a spoiled table wine is to buy it from a store that enjoys rapid turnover of its stock. In other words, get it from a merchant who sells a great deal of the specific type and brand you are buying. (At this point I am avoiding the whole subject of how some wines improve with long aging in bottles. That is covered in another chapter. Right now I am only warning against buying wines that are spoiled.)

If the bottle you contemplate selecting has a cork closure, note whether the store has kept it standing upright for a long time. In that position the cork dries out and admits air to spoil the wine. Corked bottles should be stored lying horizontally to keep the cork moist and airtight. (Bottles with screw caps can be safely kept standing up.)

It is easy to know which wines are perishable and which are not. Just look at the label, which tells the alcoholic content. You will see that the appetizer and dessert wines—like the Sherries and Ports—contain from 17 to 20 per cent alcohol, which preserves them effectively. Those are the types you can keep safely in that decanter on your sideboard. But the table wine types, usually with only 10 to 14 per cent alcohol, sometimes less, are far more delicate, suffer most when exposed to heat or even to direct sunlight, and begin to spoil soon after they are opened.

In your Bacchic shopping expeditions don't be a wine snob. You may be amazed to discover how delicious some of the lower-priced wines can be. There is no direct, inevitable relationship between a wine's price and its drinking quality. Unlike the situation among automobiles and most other kinds of merchandise, the flivvers among wines often taste better than the Cadillacs. This is especially likely to be the case when the highest-priced table wine in the store has stood overlong on the top shelf waiting for a buyer; it may be completely ruined and worthless. It sometimes happens that the most delectable wine in the entire stock is lurking on the bottom shelf, behind an unpretentious label, and bears one of the lowest price marks in the whole establishment. Take pride in the taste bargains you discover!

This is a good point at which to digress briefly—assuming you already know the type of wine you want—to discuss choosing among brands. For example, a store may offer the same kind of wine under two different brands at the same or similar prices. Other things being equal—both brands seeming to sell with equal frequency in this particular store—which should you buy?

Usually the better choice is the brand whose label shows the wine was bottled at the winery where it was made. On a French label, look for the words *mise en bouteille au château,* or similar legend that clearly means the same thing. On an American wine, various other legends, such as "Produced (or made) and bottled by," "Bottled at the winery," or "Estate bottled," convey similar messages. The usual German terms are *Originalabfüllung, Originalabzug,* and *Wachstum.* Other countries have no standard terms for this purpose.

The way to detect a wine that has *not* been bottled where it was made is to compare the address of the bottler with the appellation of origin. If the bottler's address on the label is a town in Arkansas, and the wine is called "California Burgundy," it obviously was not bottled where it was made.

Again, however, I advise experimenting, regardless of where the wine was bottled or of its price; because I know of at least two bottlers in leading American cities who are currently offering inexpensive locally bottled wines which are just as good as most of the winery-bottled products available in their localities; and some of the leading European shippers bottle uniformly good wines, while some vineyard owners do not.

Once you have found the wine whose taste thrills you,

the thing to do is run, don't walk, to the same store where you got it, and buy a few more bottles from the same lot. This is good advice because if you wait a few months to buy another bottle, it may not taste the same. Remember that few wineries are able to supply unchanging flavor and aroma in their products from month to month, much less from year to year.

Don't buy too much at a time, however. The quantity depends on how soon you are going to use it, and whether you have a cool place away from the furnace and sunlight in which to store it, with corked bottles lying on their sides. You should not buy a larger bottle of table wine than you are likely to use up within a day or two after it is opened. If you have a partially filled bottle of this low-alcohol-content wine left over from dinner, put it into your refrigerator; it will keep longer there.

A "fifth" (4/5 quart) of table wine ordinarily serves two, three, or four people at a meal. It is by far the most popular size. Experience tells you when to graduate to larger containers.

A connoisseur of my acquaintance, who enjoys red wine with his dinner nightly, but whose wife prefers milk, buys Cabernet only in half bottles, one of which he consumes at a sitting; but he usually gets a case at a time.

Incidentally, wine is cheaper by the case, which contains twelve bottles or twenty-four half bottles. Most stores will give you 10 per cent off the per-bottle price. Ask them if it isn't so, because they seldom advertise it.

Most American wines are bottled in either "fifths" or

quarts. But European table wines frequently come in somewhat smaller bottles; sometimes they hold only ¾ quart or even an ounce less. So note the net contents before you buy, to see whether you are getting your money's worth.

The best bargains in wine drinking are the half-gallon and gallon jugs that you find in practically all wine stores. Only American wines come in these particular economy sizes, but some Italian wines are sold in large *fiaschi,* and you sometimes find French wines in magnums, which are double the size of a "fifth."

Here is an additional economy tip: to get the by-the-gallon price and still protect your table wine from spoiling, transfer the contents of a gallon jug into ten screw-capped half bottles, carefully washing and drying them first; and keep them in the refrigerator until time for use.

I am often asked what quantities a host should buy for a club banquet or a large party. For this I have developed a formula from long experience. For weddings, I allow a bottle of Champagne (slightly more than six four-ounce glasses) for every three persons, unless the guests include many teetotalers, in which circumstance a bottle will serve six. For pre-dinner Sherry pouring, a bottle will provide a little more than twelve two-ounce servings. With a second helping for each, the bottle thus takes care of six people.

At a mixed-company banquet, no matter how many different table wines are on the menu, I allow an over-all average of one bottle for every four persons, and expect to need a larger quantity of the first wine served than of those that follow. But if it is to be a full-course dinner for an all-male group of connoisseurs, I calculate pre-dinner Champagne consumption at a third of a bottle per man, assorted table wines at a half bottle each, and dessert wine at a bottle for every half-dozen men. I have attended dinners, however, at which the total wine consumption averaged two bottles per guest and from which everyone walked to his taxicab with a perfectly steady gait! This can happen only when wine is consumed with rich food.

But returning to the subject of ordinary purchases, there are seven prime secrets of successful wine shopping: Experiment freely, because it is fun and inexpensive. Give your guests a choice among wines. Buy small bottles at first. Try the inexpensive as well as the more costly wines. Buy at stores which have not kept the wine too long; be sure it is in good condition. When you find a wine you like, buy some more of the same, but only the quantity you can store safely. And finally, once again this reminder: if you are going to trust a dealer to select your wine purchases for you, be sure to pick one who regularly drinks wine himself.

CHAPTER 5

WHAT'S THE BEST WINE?

WHEN YOU CORNER A WINE EXPERT and demand an answer to that oftenest asked of all vinous questions, "What's the best wine?" you usually get this reply: "The best wine is the wine you like best; you are the only expert on your individual taste."

Don't blame him for being evasive. His answer is the only one that makes any sense.

What you really want, it seems to me—and I therefore presume to rephrase your question—is to know which country or which viticultural region produces the wines that genuinely impartial experts (if any such individuals actually exist) would regard as the best of their kind in the world. This chapter will attempt to answer that knotty question.

It is true that no self-anointed authority can tell you what to like. One of the strangest aspects of viniana in America is that so many depend on the opinion of so few as to what is good. The Latin author of the saying *"de gustibus non est disputandum"* ("there is no disputing tastes") was almost surely referring to wine. Certain consumers in eastern seaboard states, who regularly made wine at home during the prohibition era, still reject any vintage that does not taste of bitter grape stems. I recall reading that Frederick the Great liked Champagne in his coffee with a bit of mustard stirred in, and that Columbus often put salt in his wine. A Greek wine called Retsina, which is flavored with resin, enjoys a considerable market in the United States, and some is produced annually in California for the Greek-American trade.

When it comes to food, Philadelphians like scrapple; haggis, the recipe for which would make you gag, is loved in Scotland; Hawaiians relish poi; the French enjoy broiled snails, and steak *tartare* is popular in Germany. The raw fish liked in Japan is easier to take than the grits and chicory-flavored coffee often encountered in our southern states.

These fascinating examples are cited to warn you that your taste is more likely to differ than to agree with the verdicts of wine experts. For virtually all of the world's wine authorities idolize the traditional wines of Europe, where some grapes are still crushed with the feet. In fact, I will show, a few pages hence, that if you were the jury, and if your preference matched that of the majority of Americans, you would award the "best wine" medals to wines the international experts would reject as differing from their centuries-old standards.

There has never been an international judging in which all of the world's best-known wines were compared, with their labels hidden, solely on their individual merits. Since such a competition is not likely to be held, I am going to venture as to how I believe it would result. My imaginary jury for this imaginary quality sweepstakes will consist of the several hundred Europe-minded oenophiles whom I have interviewed, and with whom I have tasted wines, during the past quarter of a century. Some of them, if they read the results that follow, might even agree with my awards.

France would surely receive the grand prix for *vinifera* Champagne, Sauternes, and red Burgundy.

Germany would win all the Oscars for White Rieslings.

Spain and Portugal would walk away with the *flor* Sherry and Port awards, respectively.

Italy could not be denied the medal for Sparkling Muscat, nor the prize for Chianti.

California would triumph with the world's greatest Cabernet Sauvignon, Pinot Blanc and Chardonnay, Rosé, and "madeirized" (baked) Sherry.

Each region would obviously excel with its exclusive specialties: the Island of Madeira with the wine of that name; New York, Ohio, and Ontario with their *labrusca*-flavored Champagnes and table wines; California with its Zinfandel, Emerald Riesling, and new specialty wines.

Chile, South Africa, Hungary, Yugoslavia, Greece, and Australia, if they entered the contest, might snag a few prizes. Russia's extensive viticultural industry, of which little is known in the Western world, quite conceivably would score, too.

In a hypothetical runoff for the all-time world championship among individual bottles, regardless of type, I suspect the votes would be divided between two historic table wines of France: the fabulous 1864 vintage of Château Lafite, a red Bordeaux of the Pauillac commune; and the 1929 Romanée-Conti, a red Burgundy of the Côte de Nuits. Few if any bottles of these celebrated vintages exist today, but since at the peak of their fame they have brought prices as high as thirty-five and forty dollars per bottle, respectively, this undoubtedly meant that they were magnificent nectars indeed. I have the greatest respect for the individual great wines of Bordeaux, in particular, having tasted some that deserved the most reverent praise. Meanwhile the Romanée-Conti vineyard has been uprooted and replanted; and while I do not differ with any of the quality rankings cited in recent paragraphs, the few Romanée-Conti vintages which I have sampled in the United States would win no prizes from me.

Now that Europe-minded experts have cast their ballots by proxy, let us see how Americans have voted in fact. For in the United States, during 1956, 1957, and 1958, there actually were held more than seventy "blind" wine tastings in which California wines were pitted against their counterparts among the most famous wines of Europe. The California wine industry, confident that its wines would not fare badly in objective comparisons, sponsored the tastings.

With their labels carefully concealed, hundreds of bottles of wine made in California were lined up against hundreds of bottles representing the best-known vintages of France, Germany, Italy, Switzerland, Hungary, Spain, and Portugal. Most of these had been purchased at random from store shelves.

Nearly fifteen hundred American consumers, recruited from the ranks of editors, home economists, importers, film personalities, businessmen, restaurateurs, wine merchants, government officials, the membership of wine and food societies and similar groups, were invited to taste and to write their preferences on secret ballots. The results of the first sixty-eight tastings are as follows:

Over-all point scores: California, 18,913; Imports, 18,442.

Champagnes: California, 4,113½ points; French, 3,955½ points.

Burgundies: California, 1,340½ points; French, 1,232½ points.

Other red table wines: California, 5,724½ points; Imports, 5,446½ points.

White table wines: Imports, 3,499½ points; California, 3,227½ points.

Rosés: Imports, 2,336½ points; California, 2,335½ points.

Sherries: California, 2,033½ points; Spanish, 1,829½ points.

Ports: Portuguese, 142 points; California, 138 points.

Average retail prices for the still wines tested—Imports,

$3.74; California, $1.61. For the Champagnes—Imports, $8.08; California, $4.16.

There were many red faces as results were unveiled. An importer downgraded his own merchandise. A woman who always insisted there was one white wine she preferred above all others discovered with horror that she had scored it below a humble California contender.

The sixty-eight blind tastings were held in such cities as New York, Boston, Washington, Baltimore, New Orleans, St. Louis, Milwaukee, Chicago, Houston, Los Angeles, and San Francisco. The French Government, meanwhile, was emitting well-modulated screams of indignation at the irreverence of American vintners who presumed to challenge the centuries-old reputation of Gallic winegrowers for producing the only truly fine wines in the world. At one point the French suggested that the tastings were obviously unfair because the tasters were not allowed to read the labels before voting their preferences! The French Embassy successfully brought pressure, through the Department of State, to prohibit the California vintners from advertising the shocking results, but this did not muzzle the American press, which merrily published the scores in complete detail. At this writing the comparative tastings were still going on.

I hasten to offer some excuses for the European losers. They were competing for the flavor preferences of groups predominately American. Residents of this country eat, drink, and generally live differently from those of Europe, and it is to be expected that American tastes will differ. The blind-tasted foreign wines might have included some bottles stored too long in retail outlets; although on this score the same would probably have been true of some of the California samples. What the tastings really prove is that you are more likely to enjoy a California wine bought in the United States than a foreign wine purchased here, and that, moreover, the California products give you more satisfaction for the prices you pay for them.

Note that the European wines were all high priced, presumably the Old World's finest. You wonder what the scores would be if California vintages were pitted against the cheaper imports which flooded United States markets following World War II, underselling many American wines.

Let us make some closer comparisons.

Vineyards in California's leading table-wine districts, such as Napa, Sonoma, Livermore, Santa Clara, and Santa Cruz, receive more hours of sunshine per season than the top French and German districts. More sunshine means lower acidity and higher sugar content in the grapes, which, in turn, means that California wines are less tart than the European but are higher in alcoholic content. Europe-minded judges prefer the tart French Champagne. The American blind tasters prefer the softer California version.

French red Burgundy often contains added sugar and other flavoring and coloring. At its best it is like no other beverage created anywhere. I suspect the French Burgundies' tendency toward sweetness accounts for the higher scores registered by their California counterparts, which are the pure product of the grape, and unsweetened; California regulations strictly forbid the addition of sugar.

Probably the tasters' preference for other California red wines over the imports can be credited to the state's Cabernets. California's red table-wine districts seem to provide an ideal home for the Cabernet Sauvignon grape, more so than does its original home in Bordeaux, where plantings of this noble variety have been sharply reduced since World War I.

Perhaps the imports' low total score for these red wines can be blamed on the Italian Chiantis. While this Italian type, at its best, has never been duplicated anywhere, it has had a miserable record of arriving in American homes and restaurants in spoiled condition. The one Italian wine in which I have never been disappointed is Asti Spumante (Sparkling Muscat), which has yet to be equaled in California.

The high scores of the European white table wines probably can be credited to French Sauternes and German Rhine wines.

Sauternes made in France have an extra, pleasing, non-grape flavor which few California wines possess. This flavor comes from a mold, called the *botrytis cinerea* or *pourriture noble,* which grows on overripe grapes in Bordeaux (and also exists in the Rhineland). This reminds me of the New York wine salesman who once read a book and, enthralled by his newly acquired knowledge, announced to all and sundry that the best wines are made from moldy grapes! This "noble mold" seldom grows naturally in California. Experts usually choose the French Sauternes; in this case, you might, too.

German Rhine wines, made from the White Riesling grape, are not only more tart and less alcoholic than those grown in California, but have a glycerin-like smoothness which California Rieslings still seem to lack.

Among dry white types, California's Pinot Blanc and Chardonnay wines usually cannot be distinguished from French White Burgundies; but I understand the latter scored higher than California Chablis (White Burgundy) in the tastings.

As for Rosé wines, the Europeans created this type long ago, but California, which began its production only recently, somehow seems to make it better. Foreign Rosés are usually drier than their American counterparts, which may explain the almost equal scores.

Spanish Sherry is made from grapes crushed by the shoes of dancing men called *pisadores* (steppers), but I doubt if this contributes to the flavor. The "nutty" or *rancio* taste of this Spanish wine comes from a film yeast, called *flor,* which grows on the surface in a partially filled cask. While California makes some of these *flor*-type Sherries, that state produces mainly Sherries of the "madeirized" type. made "nutty" by aging at warm temperatures. Current evidence is that Americans generally prefer the madeirized flavor to the *flor* type.

Portuguese Ports are usually older and heavier bodied than their California counterparts. The low scores reported for both indicate that not many of the tastings included this type.

But why all the emphasis on California, whose winegrowing history dates back only to 1769? Why not consider the eastern states, where Lord Delaware launched the industry in 1616, and the Midwest, where Ohio's Catawba wine was praised in Longfellow's poem? The answer is that California, besides growing more than three fourths of the wine consumed in the nation, is the only state whose wines can be compared directly to the European, being made from the same grapes—the true wine grapes, the *Vitis vinifera*. In the rest of the United States, the principal grapes grown are of the *Vitis labrusca*, varieties of American wild grapes, and mostly "foxy" in flavor. *Labrusca* wines, when well made from the choicest of these grape varieties, are delicious and have not been duplicated anywhere else in the world.

A double kinship exists between American and European wines. Cuttings of the Old World's grapevines were transplanted to California; and most vines in Europe are grafted on roots of wild American vines, transplanted from this country to combat the Phylloxera vine pest.

California has two advantages over Europe—long, rainless summers in which wine grapes manage to mature every year, and the will to apply modern scientific controls and mechanical equipment to winegrowing. Most Europeans are content to continue making wine in the time-honored but primitive ways of their ancestors.

Between its snow-covered mountains and its torrid deserts, California has many different climates and can produce every type of wine made anywhere else in the world. Yet California can no more produce a German Rhine wine or a Bordeaux Claret than Germany or France can duplicate California Rhine wine or California Claret. All wines are individuals, with the character of each vineyard's different climate and soil evident in their flavor.

It is in average quality—I should say weighted average quality, considering the mere one hundred and ninety million gallons which the United States has been making each year compared to the more than three-billion-gallon annual production in Europe—that this country is farthest ahead of the Old World. Much of the *vin ordinaire* of France, Italy, Spain, and Portugal would be considered substandard under the minimum quality regulations of the state of California, which enforces the strictest such standards in the world. Since the early years following the end of national prohibition, virtually all wines produced in the United States have at least been sound, and the bulk of American production has been far superior to the wines the average Frenchman, Italian, Spaniard, or Portuguese gets to drink with his daily meals. As long ago as 1867 California growers were shipping their wines to Germany, Denmark, England, and Canada, where they competed successfully with the wines of continental Europe. Today, by and large, American wines are better and more reliable than the wines of the Old World.

Why is it, then, that the most fashionable beverage stores in New York and other cities mainly feature imports on their shelves, even hiding their American wines from the shopper's view? There are at least three reasons. First, such a store usually derives a higher profit from the sale of an expensive foreign wine than from the home-grown product; and if I were the merchant, I might be similarly influenced. Second, because of their customers' ignorance, snobbishness, or understandable desire for variety in wines, the display of imports attracts a class of wealthy patrons; the appearance of foreign labels unquestionably creates an air of prestige for the establishment. And third, most proprietors, as well as their customers, just do not happen to know that the American wines are usually better.

Undeniably, Europe offers a greater number and variety of individual superlative wines than America can. Out of the billions of gallons produced in the scores of different vineyard regions on the older continent you would expect this to be the case.

Now we come to the delicate subject of price. Here we are tackling not only the foreign-versus-American question, but also the differences between costly and inexpensive American wines. Why should this bottle cost several dollars while its neighbor is marked at a dollar or less?

The answer is, in most cases, that the expensive wine costs that much more to produce, age, bottle, ship, and sell. The grape varieties used may be costly, delicate, and hard to handle, from a vineyard that produces perhaps two tons to the acre as against as much as ten tons in another vineyard planted to a hardier, more fruitful variety. The vintner may have selected a special lot of grapes for special care. He probably made the wine from the free-run juice, the first delicate juice released from the grape, rejecting the coarser-tasting remainder, which he later pressed from the grape pulp and sold, as press wine, to be distilled into brandy. The wine may have been aged for a long period in small casks to obtain a desired flavor. It may even have been laid away in bins after bottling, to age in glass before shipment; all of which adds to the vintner's cost.

Or there may be only a small quantity of this particular famous wine, with a strong demand from connoisseurs who are willing to pay the price to get some of it.

On the other hand, some wineries are more efficient than others, and by using scientific quality controls, mass production, and mass marketing, are able to deliver at moderate prices wines you might not distinguish, if you removed the labels, from more expensive wines.

The small winery sometimes bottles a cask of unusually fine wine under a special label. The large winery blends its best casks with the rest to give you uniformly good wine even if not so high in peaks of quality.

Then there is the romance of historic little vineyards,

their storied, castle-like wineries, and the cultivation of their vines by hand labor, which elements—when you associate them with the wine—add remarkably to its delicious taste. Europe is far richer in this respect than the vineyards of the New World.

A large vintner, discussing this element with me at dinner in his home one evening, said: "No doubt about it, the buggy was more romantic than the Chrysler Imperial; but does anyone want to trade his Chrysler for a buggy?" While he spoke, I noted that the wine on his table came from one of the romantic little wineries of California.

In this country the expensive wines are more desired than, say, expensive cigarettes. One reason is that Americans are generally suspicious of anything alcoholic that is low in price. A vintner of my acquaintance, whose wines were moderately expensive, decided to expand his business, and reduced his prices. His customers became suspicious, and his sales dropped instead of increasing.

Another reason is wine snobbery. We need no psychoanalyst to tell us that the wine we serve, like the car we drive or the home we live in, is often selected to impress others with our economic position and our discriminating taste.

If you have a fixation against snobbery, or if you enjoy discovering bargains more than you enjoy pretending that everyday articles are not good enough for you, I recommend that you experiment as follows. Buy an American wine and an import of comparable type. Mask the labels, or, better yet, switch the contents between the two bottles, serve them to your guests, and see which they prefer. The results may embarrass some of your wine-snob friends, but think of what you will add to their education!

What constitutes quality in wine, anyhow?

To the proprietor of the average grocery store in France (where most of the wine is sold), a wine's alcoholic content is the index of its worth; the greater the wine's strength, the higher the price he charges for it.

To the expert judges at wine-quality competitions, the principal criteria of a wine's quality are its freedom from certain defects, some of which are unnoticeable by the average consumer; its balance between acidity and sweetness; its aroma, and—importantly—its conformance to the wine industry's arbitrarily established specifications of color, dryness or sweetness, and grape variety flavor for the type name on its label.

To Dr. Albert J. Winkler, the great California professor of viticulture, the distinction between an ordinary wine and a fine wine is longevity—the degree to which the latter has the capacity to improve with aging. To him, improvement means two things: the development of mellow smoothness, and the natural formation of the winey perfume known as "bouquet" or "nose." These latter points do represent the aesthetic overtones of quality which evoke ecstatic praise from seasoned connoisseurs; and I am inclined to go along part of the way with Dr. Winkler. Yet many wines which are not long-lived, and which therefore do not meet his definition, are thrillingly delicious and richly aromatic with the fragrant perfumes of the grapes from which they are made.

None of these criteria quite answers the question of what constitutes wine quality.

I prefer to think that since wine is a beverage made to be enjoyed, the best wine is the one which delivers the most in enjoyment for you—a highly personal matter for your taste alone.

CHAPTER 6

KINDS FOR EVERY USE

AMONG ALL THE BEVERAGES OF mankind no other offers as bounteous a variety of flavors and uses as wine does. To quote the otherwise matter-of-fact language of the *Wine Handbook Series:*

"Wine is the one beverage that is fittingly used to celebrate the holy Mass, to accompany the workman's meal, to observe a memorable occasion, to inspire the poet, to minister to the sick, to welcome guests who drop in, to enhance the flavor of cooking, to mix drinks that cool the hot summer day or warm the cold winter evening, to make the connoisseur's banquet perfect, to launch ships, to toast beggar or king. No other beverage has had such universal recommendations through the ages."

This somewhat flowery tribute once brought me a telephone call from an impatient *Handbook* reader. "I'm not launching a ship or celebrating anything," the lady complained. "My husband's old-fogy boss, who likes your stuff, is coming to dinner tonight. Just tell me in one word or less the kind of wine I've got to buy." I prescribed a bottle each of Sauterne and Burgundy, and silently thanked the lady for teaching me thereafter to keep my wine recommendations less ambiguous, and to suggest, instead, specific wines for specific uses.

This chapter is addressed, of course, to the new wine consumer. If you have not yet discovered the many different ways in which wines can add richly to your pleasure, the suggestions that follow will be helpful.

To begin with, I advise you to buy an all-purpose wine, and to let the rest come naturally. Such an all-purpose beverage is the pink table wine called Rosé (pronounced Ro-ZAY). Frank Schoonmaker, the importer-wine author who first popularized this type in the United States, deserves the undying gratitude of American consumers for doing so. Rosé is the one wine you can bring out of your refrigerator and serve at any time for any use without a brow-wrinkling thought as to whether you have made an acceptable choice. Chill, open, and pour; it is that simple.

And since I know from experience that most readers actually enjoy reading intricate wine-serving advice, I shall offer a number of additional prescriptions. Let us start with your before-dinner hour of relaxation. The traditional pre-meal wine is Sherry. I often wonder why otherwise hospitable hosts always ask their guests "Bourbon or Scotch?" when it would be so much more considerate to say "Bourbon, Scotch, or Sherry?"

To find your Sherry preference, try several, starting with the dry kind and stopping at the point of sweetness that pleases your palate. It may turn out to be the sweet ("cream") type. Thereafter, keep a bottle handy in the refrigerator, unless you prefer it over a cube of ice, or even unchilled.

But variety adds spice, so perhaps you would like to experiment with something besides Sherry. Try Vermouths, both dry and sweet; you may like them even better. Still another idea is to mix a little Sweet Vermouth with your Sherry; this is one of my personal likes. I arrived at this after starting with the famous Bamboo Cocktail, which is two parts Sherry and one part each of Dry and Sweet Vermouth, and a dash of Angostura bitters, stored a few days in the refrigerator to blend. Then I discovered that the Sherry-Vermouth mixture alone tasted just as good.

In spite of the widespread impression that before-dinner drinks must be "dry," I insist that there is nothing wrong with sweet appetizers. If you have traveled in Europe, you know perfectly well that sweet *apéritifs* are the favorites in France and Italy. I know many people who like a glass of Port at cocktail time, or who take one of the sweet wine specialties, such as Dubonnet and the flock of new flavored *apéritif* wines, most of which, for some reason, bear the names of assorted birds or other titles which delicately suggest that a sip will send the consumer flying.

How about something extra glamorous, when you have guests at cocktail time? Here my choice is Champagne. But if that seems too expensive (which it isn't, really), and if you have a few days' warning and would like to serve a cocktail with a minimum of bother, try the A. R. Morrow recipe. Mix equal parts of Sherry, Dry Vermouth,

Sweet Vermouth, Sauterne, or any other white wine, and brandy; store in the refrigerator for a few days, and you have a drink that none of my guests, including the most hardened whisky drinkers, has ever failed to praise.

Enough about before-meal drinking; now how about ornamenting the family meal? If you won't settle for all-purpose Rosé, place a small bottle each of any red and any white dinner wine on the table and let your folks help themselves. What kinds? Any kinds! Repeat this often enough, and preferences among specific types will soon emerge.

Let's go on to the holiday or guest dinner, where ice water is never enough; these must be made really festive occasions.

For guests I usually bring out the fancy, expensive labels in my cellar; and since wine is my particular hobby, I like to match the wine exactly with the main dish. What the Wine and Food Society sometimes does is to appoint a committee, which first holds a pilot dinner; the committee members have the entire test meal served while they taste different wines with each course and make their selections for the future Lucullan feast. You needn't go to any such lengths, of course. If your main dish is to be red meat, serve any traditional dry red dinner wine—Burgundy, Cabernet, any of that group. If it is to be fish or fowl, serve any white dinner wine. Better yet, put both kinds on the table, just as I have suggested for the family meal, and you cannot go wrong. Add Rosé while you are at it, and you have insurance that your guests will be delighted.

Want your dinner to be supremely festive? Then, instead of the still wines, offer a choice of Champagne and Sparkling Burgundy.

An extra fillip, to backtrack a course or two, is to serve a special wine with the soup. This presents no problem: the wine that goes with any soup—so well, indeed, that the best canned soups already contain some—is Sherry.

When it comes to dessert, the choice is also easy, because most desserts are sweet, and so are dessert wines such as Port, Tokay, Muscatel, Cream Sherry, and the various berry wines. If you happen to encounter an especially delicious, extra-sweet Sauterne, you will enjoy that with dessert, too.

The members of my family like assorted cheeses at the end of a meal. We find that some of our guests enjoy a hearty dry red wine as the accompaniment, while others prefer red Port.

Moving on to the bridge table, which also gets exercise some afternoons, there are many wines to sip between bids. Cool White Port, Cream Sherry, the sweet Concord and berry wines, and those flavored specialties already mentioned are all especially popular here. A mixture of White Port and lemon juice became the standard afternoon bridge drink in one California suburban community a few years back.

For guests who just drop in casually, afternoon or evening, the bridge-table beverages will also do. In hot, stuffy summer weather, however, I serve them either chilled Rosé or a Wine Cooler. The latter can be anything you feel like mixing, from the simple *spritzer* (white wine and seltzer) to wine lemonade (lemonade with red wine or Rosé added), to the various wine punches for which the Wine Advisory Board prints numerous recipes that you usually can pick up at your beverage store. In recent years many people have discovered that any wine can be mixed with any kind of sweet soda pop (especially the lemon-flavored ones) and served as a delicious light highball.

Wine for the barbecue is easily chosen. Again it is Rosé or any red dinner wine. If you prefer to serve white wine with those sizzling, charcoal-broiled chickens, bring out a tub of ice to keep the bottles well chilled in hot weather.

The amazing versatility of wine extends to cold winter nights also. A traditional warmer-upper in the ski country is hot mulled wine: sweetened red wine spiced with cloves and lemon peel, warmed and served with cinnamon sticks. Get the recipe from the Wine Advisory Board, San Francisco. Also available are hot buttered wine, Sherry Tom and Jerry, and others for this purpose.

How about quantity punches for parties? The best known, of course, is Champagne Punch. But here I protest; there can be no excuse for wasting good Champagne in a mixture where this effervescent wine loses its identity and where bubbles can be gotten much more cheaply from sparkling water. Use still wines to mix the punch; then add club soda, and finally a single bottle of Champagne for the use of its glamorous name. Punch recipes, with ingredients such as sherbets, frozen concentrates, canned juices, and fresh fruits, are available by the score.

But aren't there also specific wines which fit certain uses better than all other types do? Indeed there are! For example, the one wine to sip while puffing a fragrant Havana cigar is red Port. If it had not been for the time-honored British custom of after-dinner Port for the gentlemen, while the ladies retired from the table, the Portuguese Port industry would not be what it is today.

While history fails to record the specific wine type with which ladies of Elizabethan times bathed their faces to improve their complexions, we do know that Anna Held's legendary wine bath could only have been had in Champagne. And Lucien B. Johnson, the champion wine salesman of the years immediately preceding prohibition, always insisted that the wine with which to woo a lady is not Champagne. "Champagne only makes folks talkative," Lucien used to say, "but Burgundy, warmed to the temperature of the room, makes people affectionate. Yes, Burgundy is the *only* love wine!"

You cannot marry off your daughter respectably these days without serving Champagne at the reception. Here I usually suggest to the bride's parents that they buy the least expensive kind, because the caterers always hide the labels with napkins, anyway. This also applies to ship launchings, where the Champagne is wasted.

At the Jewish holiday feasts the wine that flows must be *Kosher l'Pesach,* but fortunately the rabbis' *hechsher* seals are placed on a complete variety of wine types, so that the celebrants do have a choice.

For the sick, the oftenest-prescribed wine seems to be Port, which is also the base for some of the proprietary medicines sold in drugstores, including some of the old-time favorite tonics. This type again gets the call in the pleasant custom of laying down a bottle of wine when a child is born, to age until his twenty-first birthday.

And completing the round of the clock, Port is also the favorite nightcap wine, because of its ability to induce a pleasant night's sleep.

But wait! How about morning wines? It would be a grave omission indeed to skip Champagne breakfasts and Sunday brunches. For the former, serve a choice of white and pink Champagnes. For the latter, although Rhine wines and Champagne are both popular, I personally like the dash of color that Rosé adds.

And speaking of wine in the morning, there was once a famous connoisseur who always began the day by brushing his teeth with Sauterne.

Perhaps you now expect to find, upon turning the next page, one of those charts often found in beverage stores, dictating exactly which wines should accompany each course of a meal. It isn't there. I have been preaching for twenty-five years that nobody needs those formidable charts. They misguide instead of helping, and by their complexity they have actually discouraged millions of would-be consumers from even attempting to serve wine.

Banish any fear that you might serve a *wrong* kind of wine—unless you happen to be completely taste blind. Do you need a chart to tell you not to serve candy with steak? Of course not! Likewise you need no detailed instructions to suggest one of the sweet wines with a sweet dessert. You certainly would not serve dry, tart Claret with your *crêpes suzette*—not if you have ever tasted Claret, that is.

In all my experience I have found only one popular American main-course dish with which almost any of the traditional table wines would not blend successfully. That is the time-honored sweet-garnished Easter baked ham. The dry, puckery *red* table wine types do seem to clash with this Easter dish and the dry whites are overpowered by it. But all-purpose Rosé enhances ham's flavor wonderfully; and so does sweet Sauterne.

Of course there are certain classic taste harmonies between certain wines and certain foods. Just as coffee goes with doughnuts, mustard with hot dogs, or maple syrup with hotcakes—so the hearty red wines blend with the flavors of steaks and roasts. Likewise, white table wines with their characteristic acidity have the virtue of breaking down the sometimes unpleasant oily substances which give some sea foods their fishy flavors. That, incidentally, is the main reason why pieces of lemon are usually served with fish. And once you discover the exquisite taste harmony of ruby-red Port with walnuts you will never again reach for your nutcracker without first bringing out that particular wine.

So, instead of printing a chart of mandatory wines with different meal courses I list as follows some of the delightful taste harmonies of wines and foods known to the world's leading gourmets. With each dish I mention one or two classes of wine. Any of the specific types which are grouped under those headings in the chapter entitled "Wine Unraveled" will answer the purpose.

Shellfish—Any dry white wine.
Other fishes—Dry or semi-sweet white wines.
White-meated fowl—Any white table wine.
Red-meated fowl—White or red table wine.
Chinese foods—Any semi-sweet white table wine.
Candied baked ham—Rosé or semi-sweet white wine.
Steaks, roasts, chops, pastes—Dry red wines.
Desserts and fruits—Any sweet wines.
Cheeses—Dry red or sweet red wines.
Nuts—Red Port.

These are harmonies disclosed by noting the taste preferences of millions of people—in other words, the liking of the majority. But taste is individual; the man who likes Claret with strawberry shortcake is only in the minority—he is not wrong. For himself he is right.

CHAPTER 7

RITUAL—RIDICULOUS BUT ENJOYABLE

WHAT WE AMERICANS MEEKLY accept as compulsory rules for our service of wine would be amusing if it were not that the very existence of such rules discourages many people from introducing this civilized beverage into their homes. Fear of committing some grave social error, such as by pouring Rhine wine into the Burgundy glass or wrapping the napkin around the bottle counterclockwise when it should go the other way, causes many a host and hostess to serve their guests palate-paralyzing highballs before dinner instead of accompanying the meal with wine, which could enhance the flavor of the food.

This is all the more distressing when it is realized that some of the wine rules slavishly obeyed in the United States are as garbled in translation from their common-sense Old World origins as the spelling of French dishes' names on the average American restaurant menu. The available tomes on etiquette give conflicting wine advice, and the clumsy way in which wine is mishandled by the average American waiter would be laughable if it were not so pitifully burdensome on both waiter and patron.

The obvious solution for Americans in general, as the happy alternative to obeying a ritual which has been made ridiculous by distortion, is to serve wine as simply as we do water, beer, or Coca-Cola. That is how wine is served in millions of homes in the wine countries of Europe; bottle and glasses are placed on the table, and the host pours for the guests or lets them help themselves. This is more nearly correct than the gymnastics currently performed in thousands of homes and dining establishments in this country.

The connoisseurs who make a hobby of stern conformance to rigid wine-serving customs sometimes go to ludicrous extremes. For example, at a gay party in an eastern city a gentleman paid his lady the highest of compliments by drinking Champagne out of her slipper; and she, being thrilled, drank his health in return. A critic, who happened to know of an ancient taboo, denounced her for drinking out of her own slipper, and her shocking action received wide publicity.

Fortunately, such arbiters of what is correct on bibulous occasions are few, and the authorities usually display their wine knowingness to one another in their own exclusive circles, seldom bothering the rest of us.

On the other hand, there is no denying that ceremony adds something to the pleasure of having wine. This is the one beverage whose rich heritage of tradition and symbolism affords the opportunity for gracious, formal service. Toasts to your guests' health can be drunk in malt or spirituous liquors, too, but only wine provides an excuse for ceremonial rites at the dinner table. Moreover, many of us enjoy pomp and ritual—which, by the way, undoubtedly helps to account for the popularity of many fraternal organizations. Formal wine service can be fun but is no more compulsory than white tie and tails; and your unwillingness to fuss with it should not prevent you from enjoying wine.

There are in the world of American connoisseurs and wine snobs a dozen cardinal rules of ostentatious wine service. Silly or otherwise, they are: (1) correct stemware, (2) correct table setting, (3) no smoking, (4) decanting, (5) correct wine temperature, (6) napkin around bottle, (7) cutting the capsule, (8) drawing the cork, (9) smelling same, (10) "pouring the cork," (11) order of service to guests, (12) correct wine with each course.

Taking these rules one by one, let us attempt to make some sense out of them.

As for correct stemware, I suggest that you first get rid of those pretty wineglasses you received as a wedding gift. They may look lovely displayed on a shelf, but, with certain exceptions, they are worse than useless for drinking wine. Why? Because the wine-ignorant manufacturers make them in thimble sizes that don't hold enough wine for more than a taste. When you serve a guest the skimpy two-ounce portion that the average one of these baubles holds, he empties it at a single sip and waits, thirsty and embarrassed, for you to pour some more.

In Europe you are served table wine in respectable stemmed bowls that hold seven, eight, or even nine ounces. Rarely are they poured more than two-thirds full; the head space allows the wine to send forth its fragrance, which is part of its flavor.

You will do better to serve table wine in your water goblets than in the tiny so-called wineglasses. If the water glass seems too big, pour it only half full. At a dinner in your home, four ounces of table wine is a decent serving; the average guest will have a second glass. Your old-fashioned cocktail glasses, or even your highball glasses, are equally acceptable. Or buy some of the sensible wineglasses which a few manufacturers are at last beginning to place on the market in response to the urgent pleas of vintners. The best ones are plain in design, to let the wine's color show through; they are tulip-shaped—narrower at the top than at the widest part of the bowl—thereby concentrating the wine's bouquet to delight your olfactory sense. They measure seven or eight ounces to their brim, providing a four-ounce serving when half full, and are sturdy enough to survive ordinary dishwashing. I use mine for all kinds of wine, pouring only a third of a glass when serving Sherry.

The thimbles in your set of stemware will do for cordials; or, if they can hold at least two ounces without spilling onto the tablecloth, are also suitable for serving Sherry, Port, and other dessert wines.

Whoever first inflicted on American householders the several different grotesquely shaped, various-sized and colored glasses that are sold as complete sets for the separate serving of Claret, Burgundy, Rhine wine, Sauterne, Sherry, and Port, must have copied them out of some rare old book treasured only by glassware hobbyists. In medieval Europe, it is true, every ancient winegrowing district originally developed its own distinctive wineglass. For example, the old Rhine wine glasses were colored green to hide the fact that early Rhine wines were often cloudy and brown. Such relics of past centuries are no excuse for bamboozling the average American shopper into buying ridiculous glassware.

My particular pet annoyance is the inverted-cone-shaped trinket called a Sherry glass, which cannot hold much more than an ounce and a half without spilling. When I want Sherry, I want at least two full ounces or none at all. This abominable, widely-used ornament is the reason hardly anybody ever orders Sherry in a restaurant or bar, where the price charged is excessive but the portion served in this exasperating little glass is skimpy.

Despite the foregoing tirade, it must be admitted that our eyes condition our taste buds, and that consequently wine does taste better when sipped from a thin, long-stemmed, crystal-clear glass than from a tin cup or a kitchen tumbler. You are likely to avoid the eggshell-thin, long-stemmed kinds which break too easily. But most important is to avoid the glasses that are too small to provide a decent-sized serving.

The best example of eye appeal is furnished by the hollow-stemmed Champagne glass. The tiny protuberance at the bottom of the hollow stem causes the wine's bubbles to cascade pleasingly upward long after the wine in the bowl has ceased to sparkle.

The second rule of wine ritual—correct table setting—originated with the formal banquets of an earlier century. If you have time to fuss with details, and are serving several different wines at a dinner, this provides an opportunity to put on a pretentious display of how much stemware you possess. At each diner's right place two or three glasses (no more; guests need elbow room). Each successive wine is poured into the glass closest to the table's edge. When that particular wine is finished, the glass is usually removed.

A number of hostesses have asked me whether to include the water glass when setting the table to include wine. Since Americans are habituated to ice water with their meals, it cannot very well be omitted; but I never fill the water glass unless the guest wishes it. In European homes, a bottle of water is usually available for guests who wish to dilute their wine.

Once at a banquet of gourmets, who regard water as fit only for bathing, I was surprised to see pitchers of that tasteless liquid placed in the center of the table. A closer look disclosed several goldfish swimming in each pitcher—an eloquent expression of the dinner committee's opinion on the subject.

Number three rule—that nobody may smoke where wine is being served—belongs to groups such as the Wine and Food Society and nowhere else. Except among professional wine tasters who must keep their palates keen, because their job is to detect flaws in wines rather than to enjoy them, this taboo is plainly silly. There is plenty of smoking at banquets in the wine countries of Europe.

Ritual number four, the decanting, is sometimes necessary if you are serving an extremely old red wine, in order to avoid pouring sediment into the guests' glasses. But in recent years leading vintners, both in America and in Europe, have learned to stabilize their wines before shipment; and only very rarely do you now find a bottle containing the sediment or crust (consisting of grape solids) which some wines deposit with great age. If you ever have occasion to perform the decanting rite, do it before the guests arrive. Gently pour the wine from the original bottle into a decanter in front of a candle flame. When the light discloses tiny fragments of sediment swimming by, that is the point at which to stop pouring.

Another way to avoid putting mud into your guests' glasses is to lay the venerable bottle on its side in one of those metal or wickerware wine cradles. By careful handling the contents can be poured without disturbing the sediment. It is ornamental, but unnecessary, to use a cradle to serve a wine that is perfectly clear.

Ask half-a-dozen experts at what temperature to serve a given wine and you are likely to get six different answers, some in degrees Fahrenheit or Centigrade. This makes wine seem like too much bother, and is ridiculous anyhow, because a cold wine warms while it is in your glass.

But just as most of us like our soup fairly hot and our

coke ice cold, we enjoy some wines best unchilled and others chilled. You can at least be sure that everyone wants white table wines and Champagnes cold; many of their labels tell you to serve them that way.

Tradition says to serve red wines at "room temperature," but this rule must have originated in chilly castles in England, because in the steam-heated apartments of America that would make your Burgundy lukewarm. If you do a little experimenting, you may reach the same answer most of my friends have: that most red wines are liked slightly cool, and the slightly-sweet "vinos" right out of the refrigerator.

However, if you are bringing out a bottle of *very old* red table wine, the "room-temperature" tradition is almost right. Since the main reason for aging such a wine is to develop its fragrant bouquet, it is worth bringing the bottle to the dining room an hour before dinner and removing the cork to let the wine breathe, thus releasing its winy perfume. This also helps with young red wines, if they are served at room temperature.

As for Rosés, Sherries, and white dessert wines, most people seem to like them cold, but preferences do vary. I like my red Port chilled, too.

In modern American homes the quickest way to chill a bottle of wine is to lay it in the freezer for a short time. If there is no hurry, a few hours in the refrigerator usually suffice.

Silliest of all wine customs is the napkin wrapped around the bottle. Three excuses are offered for this piece of hocus-pocus: that it prevents the hand from warming a chilled bottle (in which case, why use it for red wine?); that it prevents the bottle, wet from chilling in an ice bucket, from dripping water, and that the cloth catches any drops that might drip. Actually, the napkin is only an affectation, and an unpleasant one, because it hides the label from a guest who might like to know what he is drinking. The only good excuse for the napkin is one never mentioned: that in opening a bottle of Champagne there is a one-in-a-billion chance of the bottle breaking from the pressure inside, and the napkin protects the hand.

The best way to prevent wine from dripping on the tablecloth is to twist your wrist inward slowly as you finish pouring—thus catching any stray drops on the lip of the bottle. There are also some gadgets that you can buy to insert in the bottle's mouth for the same purpose.

Rule number seven—cutting the capsule—is a mere foible of people like me, who like the bottle to look its prettiest. Whereas most people tear off the foil or plastic that protects the cork or cap—thus making the bottle seem rather naked—the connoisseur carefully cuts it, just below the bottle's lip, before wiping the cork clean.

The next bit of ritual also makes gracious sense. It calls for the host to open the bottle at the table—not in the kitchen. There is something about the popping of the cork that whets the guests' tastes for the wine.

But ceremony number nine, in which the host deliberately smells the cork, is only disagreeable, and is made quite unnecessary by the next performance, which is called "pouring the cork."

I have often been asked why this is done—that is, why the host's first action, after the bottle is opened, is to pour an ounce or two into his own glass. There are two reasons: first, to let any bits of broken cork go into his glass in order that the guests shall not get any; and second, to allow him to taste the wine and make certain that it has not spoiled. Since a musty cork can make the wine taste "corky," this obviates the necessity of going through the smelling procedure.

Fussiness reaches an absurd climax in the eleventh piece of ritual: the exact order in which a wine is served to the guests. The books of rules are in pontifical agreement that the host must proceed counterclockwise around the table, serving first the lady at his right, then each of the other feminine guests, and next reverse his direction, serving wine to the gentlemen. I am happy to report that only once in my experience have I ever witnessed this solemn rite performed; and on that occasion I don't think anyone else even noticed. In other words, serve your guests in any order that is convenient.

As for the final rule, requiring the correct wine with each course, I trust that the discussion in the earlier chapter about kinds of wine for every use has already relieved the reader of any concern on that particular score. It would be far better if the rule makers would emphasize the fact that dry wines taste best when served before sweet wines, and white wines before the reds.

Scoring the twelve cardinal rules of wine ritual, then—here is how we stand. The correct wineglass to use is a glass that is big enough to supply a decent serving. The rigid rules of table setting, no smoking, decanting, capsule-cutting, cork-drawing, smelling, pouring and serving, and correct wine with each course, can all be safely ignored. Chill white wines and Champagnes—the rest can be chilled or not—according to how they taste best to you. And the napkin around the bottle should be abolished.

Finally, here is the secret of how to open corked bottles with a flourish instead of a struggle. Of course if you use only wines sealed with the easily-opened screw caps, you don't need this advice. But since most higher-priced wines are closed by long, straight, often stubborn corks, it is quite necessary. If you have ever suffered the ignominy of straining vainly to pull a cork with the bottle held between your knees—or of being compelled to push the pesky plug into the bottle with a pencil because the corkscrew had pulled completely through—you will especially value the following suggestion.

This is to go shopping for a good corkscrew. That implement must have two distinct virtues: good leverage and a good worm. Corkscrews on the market come with several different kinds of leverage gadgets—some quite elaborate, but all of them good. Don't let these shiny appendages hypnotize you into buying a corkscrew with an inefficient worm.

In fact, the worm—the part that goes into the cork and mustn't let go—is by far the most important part. The point of the worm must be exactly in line with its spirals; there should be an open space down the center. The worm should also be long enough to go all the way through a two-inch-long cork; and the edges should not be sharp. Never buy a corkscrew whose point is exactly in the center; if you own one of those, throw it away.

You can safely take my word for the foregoing, because in 1944 I launched a two-year Wine Institute research project, enlisting the aid of the world-famous physicist, Dr. Leonard B. Loeb, in which we tested every known shape of corkscrew and finally revealed the previously undiscovered mechanical principle involved. It is so simple that we should not have needed the tests to discover it. A sharp-edged worm with its point centered is actually an auger; it bores a hole and weakens the cork. But a worm with point and spirals in perfect alignment, and with no sharp edges, worms its way into the cork without weakening it; and when it is pulled, grips the cork from the inside and doesn't let go.

As a result of our tests dozens of manufacturers redesigned their corkscrews to conform to the foregoing specifications. However, unfortunately, not all have done so—which is why the corkscrew buyer must still beware.

CHAPTER 8

THE GREAT RESTAURANT SWINDLE

SOMEDAY IN THE ROSY, DISTANT future it will become possible for us to sip a glass of decent wine in the average American hotel or restaurant without being victimized by extortionate prices.

I also firmly predict that the time will come when we shall be able to order the brand and type we happen to like with our meal, and when the wine will be served to us unspoiled, and either cold or unchilled as it should be —as promptly as any other item on the menu.

The reasons I am certain these things will come to pass are that the public eventually gets what it wants in products and service—as witness the revolutionary changes in stores and automobiles—and that restaurateurs cannot continue for many more years to ignore the growing appreciation and demand for wine in the United States.

Until that day arrives, however, most of the millions of Americans who enjoy this civilized beverage will continue drinking it mainly in their homes; and the nation's dining places will continue swindling, with badly served wines priced at many times what they are worth, the few affluent patrons who occasionally order a bottle.

There is one way to speed the end of the present extortion and bungling. It is for us, the victimized public, to protest and keep protesting until the restaurateurs awaken to the fact that they are cheating themselves as well as their patrons.

A bottle of ordinary French wine was costing the average candle-lit New York restaurant, during 1964, somewhere between seventy cents and one dollar. Such an establishment was also buying some of the poorer foreign wines for as little as sixty cents a bottle.

In those very restaurants, however, credulous consumers were being charged from four to five dollars for the very same bottles—from four to eight times what they cost the proprietors—while equivalent wines were available at stores around the corner for $1 to $1.50.

Why has this continued? First, because we, the public, have not yet begun to complain, as we do when our soup is served lukewarm or the ice cream comes to the table melted. And second, because American restaurateurs are mainly a stubborn lot, given to aping one another, unwilling to experiment with innovations in merchandising, and unable to see that they could easily sell ten times as much wine as their present volume if their avarice were not beclouding their business sense. Preferring to sell highballs, which impair their patrons' ability to appreciate fine food, they miss the opportunity to have their menus better appreciated with the flavor-enhancing accompaniment of good wine.

The way these restaurants (they are all over America; I only use New York as an example) discriminate against the wines of this country is even more reprehensible. Many prestige establishments refuse to offer American wines at all; and in the places where the good native products are stocked they are ignominiously called "domestic" and are often listed without their brand names, while the overpriced imports are glorified. More than once a waiter has told me, when I have asked for a California or New York State brand, that it was out of stock, when he and I both knew the wine was there.

Now, it so happens that many of the best-known premium-priced American brands cost the restaurant little more than the cheap foreign items it sells. Why, then, are these top United States wines not available?

The answer is that the proprietor—because his customers are unaware of how little the cheap foreign wines cost him—gets away with charging more for them than for the American products. He knows that some of his customers are familiar with the store prices of the latter—usually around $2.00 in most cities. In other words, the restaurant reaps a much higher per-bottle profit when he sells the inferior imports. He charges for some foreign wines at 800 per cent markup, but hesitating to try extorting more than 400 per cent on the American, prefers not to sell the latter at all.

This is further evidence that the eventual remedy will

come from buyer complaints. Actual proof is the price the average restaurant charges for beer. Few places would dare to make their customers pay more than fifty to seventy-five cents for a bottle of brew, because people know how cheaply beer is priced in the supermarket.

The same kind of figuring accounts for the fact that the popular-priced wines which sell in stores for only a dollar or less are almost never available in the average hotel or restaurant. The excuse always given is that these brands are not good enough to accompany the establishment's exquisite food. The truth is that the customer has previously seen these brands' prices advertised; and the degree of restaurants' gouging is influenced by what the traffic will bear.

When the bright future of wine in United States eating places eventually dawns, it will bring several improvements in addition to fair prices. For one thing, the wine will come to our tables in better condition. At present, because so little is sold, much is being allowed to spoil by standing too long in the restaurants' overheated storerooms. In the best hotels in such cities as Washington, D.C., I have repeatedly been served white wines so oxidized that they tasted like Sherry.

This condition will naturally be remedied when stocks turn over more rapidly. Service will improve, too. One cause of the surly way waiters treat wine customers is the inefficient, inconvenient physical service setup in the average restaurant. Some places do not supply corkscrews; others store their bottles too far from the dining rooms.

It often takes so long to get a white wine chilled to accompany the diner's roast chicken that the bottle arrives in time to be poured with the dessert.

Give waiters and waitresses enough practice in serving wine and they will get over their clumsiness in doing so. They will discover that wine, which requires only the bottle, corkscrew, and glass, is far easier to serve than, for example, coffee, which involves cup, saucer, cream, and sugar; and more profitable than ice water, which does not increase the amount of their tips. Even Champagne has become less of a chore to handle with the new plastic closures that come out easily; and modern refrigeration can keep the bottles pre-chilled, so that the old-fashioned ice bucket, if used at all, becomes a mere ornament.

All of these things must happen. In fact, in our more cosmopolitan cities we already find an occasional restaurant where a bottle of good wine, well and promptly served, costs only from $2.00 to $2.75. Some of them, and a few men's clubs and better hotels, have also discovered the prestige and profit in having selected wines bottled under their own house labels at special prices. Here and there we even discover a dining place which offers table wines by the glass with meals. Whenever we contemplate dining out, such establishments deserve our patronage.

But what can we wine lovers do—when we reside in or visit a city where no such oases exist—to get a bottle of our favorite beverage with a restaurant dinner? If we are willing to engage in coaxing nasty waiters, and to be fleeced by the management in the bargain, the wine can usually be had.

The secret is to start, the moment you reach your table, a relentless campaign to get the bottle served. Ask immediately for the wine list; if none is to be had, confer with the bartender to learn what he has in stock. Make your selection, and insist firmly that the wine be brought immediately. By doing this early you may, if you are lucky, get it served in time for your main course.

Remember that a waiter's acceptance of your wine order does not mean it will be delivered. If you are not careful, he may return with your food ready to eat, and report with a smirk that the establishment is all out of the wine you ordered. This makes it advisable to select the wine and insist upon receiving it before you consent to order your dinner. Remember that if it is a white wine, it may still have to be chilled.

More than once I have had to accompany a waiter to the storeroom and help him find the bottle of my choice.

It is well to order a half bottle, to avoid being stuck with a large one if the contents happen to be bad. I dislike rejecting a faulty wine. Ordinarily I order an American brand if one is listed; and if none seems available I sometimes get it anyway, simply by asking.

Resist all attempts to foist expensive wines on you and to make you feel cheap when you order a moderately priced bottle. Remember that despite their snooty behavior restaurant personnel despise the sucker who yields to their salesmanship in behalf of costly imports. They quickly recognize the seasoned patron who orders the best bargain. Don't be afraid to seem different!

Another method that sometimes works is to ignore the waiter or waitress entirely, and to order your wine directly from the captain or the bartender. Sometimes one of these men turns out to be a Europe-trained professional, who enjoys serving this beverage, respects people who order it, and is heartily ashamed—as American restaurateurs in general ought to be—of the ineptness and extortion that mark their past treatment of wine.

And if, by fortunate chance, you occasionally succeed in getting a satisfactory wine, well served, at a price that does not represent larceny, remember to thank all of the personnel in sight. It will help to speed the restaurant wine millennium.

We lovers of wine will eventually have our way.

CHAPTER 9

WHAT VINTNERS DON'T TELL

My WINEMAKER FRIENDS often mildly wonder at the naïveté of fascinated outsiders who write admiring books about the vintner's art. To those who labor in vineyard and cellar, the growing of grapes and the fermenting of the juice into wine seem essentially simple operations. Mother Nature, after all, does the principal work; art and science are employed only to assure that Nature will do it well—that the liquid will not spoil (as it would if left untended), that the finished product will be clear, not cloudy, and that it will be as fragrant and delicious as circumstances permit.

Some of the popular misconceptions about wine, although they enhance its charm, are partly responsible for its as yet limited use in the United States, because they often lead to consumer disappointments on opening a bottle. Vintners, reluctant to dispel their customers' pleasant illusions, make little or no effort to correct them. In this respect the vintner resembles the old man in the story who, charged with seducing a lovely young woman, found the accusation so flattering that he could not resist pleading guilty.

The purpose of this chapter is to straighten out a few of the more prevalent warped impressions. One of these is the myth of old wine.

Almost everyone regards great age as the noblest of all vinous virtues. Yet most of the world's wine is consumed before it is even a year old. It is well that this is so, because the average wine, if stored for many years, will lose quality instead of improving.

The Rosés, for example, are at their peak of delicious drinking quality at about six months of age; after that point they begin losing their fresh flavor and aroma, commencing to turn brown and to taste that way. Most white table wines are likely to attain their optimum taste and fragrance within a year after vintage. The same is true of many reds.

It is the *exceptional* wines which create the age fallacy and lead poets to pen verses in praise of venerable vintages. Even some vintners are victims of this particular error and are guilty of keeping certain wines too long in cask before bottling them.

The consumer, who thinks wine has to be old to be good, asks the store clerk: "How old is this wine?"

The clerk, repeating what the vintner's salesman told him, replies: "This bottle is four years old, but that other one is six, and costs a little more." Actually, both wines might have been fermented during the previous October.

Some wine men say: "Why bother to explain? Let people think it's old; they enjoy it more."

Far be it from me to deny the marvelous improvement which aging accomplishes in certain wines, because it is true that many dessert wines gain vastly in mellowness and bouquet through the years, and that rare Clarets, such as the noble Cabernet Sauvignon, are actually undrinkable until they have matured three to five years in the cask. My own cellar contains a number of bottles ten to twenty years old, which are still improving.

But it would be far better to let the public know that most wines have only a brief life span—that each matures at a different time and thereafter fades—than to continue allowing good wines to spoil. Even in the wine countries of Europe, some of the cobwebbed bottles in restaurants' cellars are long past their prime; and in America, where purveyors are generally innocent of wine knowledge, many thousands of bottles (especially of white and Rosé table wines) are being allowed to deteriorate in stores and restaurants before they are sold.

Rather than belittle the delightful quality of long-lived wines I devote an entire section, in the later chapter for hobbyists, to the selection of those bottles whose contents do improve with the passage of years.

The only way to determine a wine's age is to look for a vintage year on the label—if there is one—and to perform a little arithmetic. Why not simply state the number of years of age, as whisky labels do? The answer is that a government regulation prohibits it, and the industry—

realizing that age is deceptive as an index of wine quality —generally approves of this taboo.

Vintage dates are a prolific source of wine confusion. In European countries, such as France and Germany, the vintage year is a mark used to identify the occasional years when the weather in the vineyard districts has been sunny enough to allow the grapes to reach full maturity. Years of bad weather, and of consequently poor wine, occur in these countries with such unpleasant frequency that the connoisseur feels compelled to learn which are the good years, simply to be able to avoid buying the bad ones.

In California, the source of most American wines, the normally long, rainless summers permit the grapes to mature fully in almost all years. It is often said that every year is a vintage year in California, although this is not entirely true, because even that sunny state sometimes suffers a period of early autumn rains. But this happens so rarely—about once in a decade—that the purpose of vintage labeling on the French and German products does not apply here.

A major objection to vintage labels is that the United States regulation requires, when a year is stated, that the wine in the bottle must have been 100 per cent grown and fermented during that year. Thus, when—as often happens —an old wine needs freshening with a blend of younger wine, the right to bear a vintage label is lost. Moreover, while this 100 per cent rule is strictly enforced in the United States, our government has no inspectors watching what happens in wineries across the Atlantic. Some French vintners have even admitted to me that their vintage-labeled wines often do contain blends of different years. Actually, considering the general lack of inspection in European wineries, there is nothing except the foreign vintner's conscience to prevent him from stretching a good vintage with a bad one.

Some of the small California winegrowing estates use vintage labels in spite of this handicap. These particular wineries do very little blending, and their products consequently vary in flavor from year to year. They need some way to identify each different bottling; and the vintage label serves this purpose for them.

A wine-store proprietor recently commented on this subject as follows: "Vintages, schmintages!" he said. "To me and my customers they're just a lot of numbers. When people ask me which years are good, I don't know, but I'm not going to admit it. So I just tell them the oldest one is the best. Now, what I want to know is, why do the wineries insist on making their stuff so complicated?"

The store proprietor's complaint is largely justified. A vintage date may occasionally help a genuine expert to identify a specific wine from a vineyard with whose reputation and products he happens to be familiar. But for the average buyer, the vintage date is not a sound guide to wine satisfaction, and should not be relied upon.

Besides, some of the finest wines are undated.

Another subject that vintners seldom discuss in public

is their cost of production, especially in comparison with the prices consumers pay for wines.

The blunt fact is that most wine is actually cheaper to produce than milk. One recent comparison showed that one gallon of milk freshly pumped from the cow costs the average dairyman nearly as much as two gallons of sound new wine are likely to cost the average winery proprietor.

Of course I refer to the least expensive table wine—fermented from grapes of standard quality, aged a few months, and ready to drink. Other wines naturally cost more to produce, such as the kinds made from rare, shy-bearing grape varieties, gently handled and matured for many years in small casks, in which their volume shrinks; and especially the dessert wines, to which the producer has added wine spirits to preserve the natural grape sugar and thus to keep the wines sweet. (In fact, it takes perhaps fourteen thousand grapes to make a gallon of dessert wine, compared to only half as many for table wine.)

In addition are the costs of bottle, cork or screw cap, label, case, and transportation. But even these, plus the profits of distributors and retailers, fall far short of accounting for the wine prices in average American stores.

The point to which I am leading is that we, the consumers, when we buy a wine, are paying a series of federal, state, and local taxes, heaped one on top of the other, several times greater than the value of the product.

From the farmer's standpoint—for wine is a product of the soil, a fruit juice usually fermented by the farmer at the vineyard—the federal gallonage tax alone, during

1964, amounted to $275 for an acre of grape land producing table wine, or $650 if the land was used for dessert wine. And some individual states charge gallonage taxes even higher than the federal rates in addition—in some cases three to six times higher.

One reason vintners discuss this subject in public on only rare occasions is that other alcoholic beverages nowadays are taxed even more; and the wine industry, in a nation which still fails to distinguish this wholesome drink from hard liquor, understandably refrains from even raising the issue.

But wine, unlike beer and distilled spirits, is primarily an article of food. To those of us who use it daily on our family dinner tables it is an integral part of our diet like bread and meat.

It is up to the consuming public, rather than to the vintners, to demand of our federal and state legislators relief from these exorbitant taxes. For the vintner does not pay them; he merely advances the money, and in the final analysis we consumers pay these taxes every time we purchase a bottle of wine.

In Portugal, where wine is recognized as food, it is subject to no excise tax whatever and a bottle accordingly costs the householder less than an equal quantity of beer. In Spain ordinary table wine is less expensive than bottled drinking water.

But the most amazing comparison between the value of a wine and the tax it pays is furnished by Champagne. In 1964 the federal tax on this sparkling wine was $3.40

per gallon—twenty times the tax on table wine. (This is something about which vintners *do* complain.)

It might be argued that Champagne, unlike Claret or Sauterne, is a luxury—the beverage for celebrating special occasions such as weddings—and should be taxed as such.

But the naked fact is that an average Champagne is really little more than a rather neutral white table wine, which you probably could not distinguish from Sauterne if it didn't contain bubbles. There is a widespread belief, obviously shared by the Congress, that this effervescent drink is one of the most intoxicating of all beverages. Yet, unless bubbles can make you giddy—which seems doubtful, since they are the same carbon dioxide that makes soda pop sparkle—this must be purely psychological, because actually Champagne contains no more alcohol than Sauterne or Claret.

Granted, there is also something special about that extra-thick Champagne bottle, its massive wired-in cork, and the jolly popping noise it makes as it flies toward the ceiling. But these, too, are purely ornamental, because the product would be equally safe in a modern crown-capped coke bottle. In other words, the government is taxing us—the public—all of those extra dollars for nothing but the bubbles.

Even more extortionate is the $2.40 per gallon federal tax on artificially carbonated wine, which is not allowed to call itself Champagne or even to be labeled "sparkling." The government is not entirely to blame for this imposition on a public that likes effervescent drinks. The producers of Champagne, fearing that bartenders preparing Champagne cocktails might substitute carbonated wine for the genuine product, have insisted that the tax on this potential competitor be kept high.

Equally unjustified is the collection of the full Champagne tax rate on the product called crackling wine, which is Champagne in which the pressure is weak and the bubbles are few.

There has been lengthy controversy on this subject of bubbles in wine. In 1958 it was partly resolved when the Congress voted to allow "still" wines to contain carbon dioxide up to five pounds per square inch pressure without being subject to any increased taxes. The consumer will not see any bubbles in such wine, but will find the taste somewhat fresher; and the keeping quality of the wine will be improved.

Something else you seldom hear mentioned by vintners is the "finishing" their products receive nowadays.

If you have ever tasted wine in a winery—I mean a sample taken directly through the bunghole by that old-fashioned gadget appropriately called a thief—you remember how remarkably delicious it tasted. You probably have noted that the same kind of wine, bought at a store and served in your home—although still an excellent drink—never had exactly the same flavor you remembered.

You were right; it was not the same. Vintners, both in America and in Europe, only wish that it could be. And generally it could, if we—the public—did not insist that every bottle we buy must be brilliantly clear. In other words, consumers' refusal to buy wines that contain natural grape sediment compels wineries to polish their products before bottling, inevitably thus losing some of their fruity flavor.

Wine, after all, is only grape juice which has preserved itself naturally by fermentation, gaining wonderful new taste and fragrance in the process. Like the unfermented grape juice sold in groceries, it contains grape solids held in suspension; and you have noted grape-juice labels (and occasionally wine labels, too) which told you to expect some of these solids to deposit in the bottle as sediment. An unfinished wine does the same; and a crust or *chemise* formed inside a bottle of very old wine is actually a mark of age and quality. In England, connoisseurs of old Ports long ago came to insist on getting crust in their bottles, until the Portuguese Port trade began to accommodate them by purposely bottling some of the wines young, in bottles with rough inside surfaces to which the crust readily clings.

But American consumers have never learned to accept sediment in wines; and as a result most of the shiny equipment you see inside today's modern wineries has nothing to do with making wine but is there primarily to filter, polish, and stabilize the liquid—to make it look and stay looking attractive.

This is not to say that wines need no clarifying. The principal function of aging, once a wine has fermented, is to let the yeasts and the heavier grape solids settle to the bottom of the cask. In new wines, you can actually taste the yeast; and after World War II, when American and German vintners came to realize that white table wines taste fresher when bottled young, consumers often noted some with a faint, but not objectionable, yeasty flavor.

Winemakers help the initial aging process by chilling their new wines or by keeping them in cool cellars; by adding clarifying agents which deposit out of the liquid, carrying unwanted solids with them; and also use additional methods, developed by modern research—such as passing the wine over ion-exchange resins to help the clarification.

Some connoisseurs like to display their vinous knowledge by denouncing all modern processing, insisting that only wines in their completely natural state can be good; and they especially disapprove of pasteurized wines. Here they reach a ridiculous extreme.

For sediment is one thing; spoilage is another. When a bottle of wine leaves the winery, it runs a gantlet of hardships which it must survive; it may have to stand in a freight car in winter-freezing temperature or desert heat; it must remain clear on the shelf of an overheated store, and still be sound and bright when you open the bottle. A delicate product of nature, it readily breaks down and clouds; and the sediment that an actually spoiled wine deposits in a bottle is not the healthy kind I have referred to earlier. To survive these conditions wine needs to be stabilized to remain sound in both heat and cold.

Vintners have not yet succeeded in finding a way to impart keeping quality to pink (Rosé) wines, which get their color by being allowed to ferment with the pulp and skins of the grapes for a short time, then being drawn off, like white wines, to complete their fermentation alone. The Rosés are the shortest-lived of all wines.

Especially subject to spoilage are the sweet table wines, which are liable to referment, and sometimes do—blowing out their corks and perfuming the premises.

There are two methods of preventing refermentation. The oldest is to "gas" the wine with sulfur dioxide, a preservative which virtually all wines contain in infinitesimal amounts far below your taste threshold. Some consumers, with unusually sensitive noses, can taste it in wines such as Sweet Sauternes. The other method is pasteurization, the same protection given to milk. Nobody has ever proved that a wine, properly pasteurized, tastes at all different from one not so protected.

Actually, while vintners treasure the romance and traditions of their ancient art and try to make their advertisements exude the atmosphere of moss-covered caves and wooden casks, grape and wine technology has been revolutionized in recent years. America and Germany lead the revolution, which fact accounts for the generally better taste and reliability of their wines, compared to those of countries such as Portugal and Spain, where grapes are still crushed by human feet to make Port and Sherry. (For Sherry, however, the men do wear shoes.)

Those who maintain that the wines of ancient Greece and Rome were the greatest, because poets praised them so highly, forget that the ancients preserved wine with pitch, resin, and salt water, and also added spices to hide the flavors of spoilage.

Wine, an industry considerably more than five thousand years old, has only enjoyed the advantages of scientific research for the past one hundred years. Such research has progressed most rapidly in the United States. Since the repeal of prohibition, the University of California, with its experimental vineyards and experimental winery and distillery at Davis, has attracted students from all parts of the world. They come to study under such professors as Amerine, Berg, Cruess, Guymon, Joslyn, Marsh, Olmo, Webb, and Winkler, to learn modern methods of growing grapes and making better wine. Important contributions have been made by the New York State Agricultural Experiment Station at Geneva, New York. In Canada, pioneering grape and wine research is conducted at the Horticultural Experiment Station and Products Laboratory at Vineland, Ontario.

An example of the unpublicized struggle between old and new is the traditional oaken cask, the pleasant, romantic symbol of old wine. Someday, before many more grape harvests have passed, the handsome casks, puncheons, butts, and barrels may be relegated to the status of mere ornaments. For it is being proved that some wines—no one has yet ventured to say all types—taste better and are more fragrant if they are never allowed to touch wood during aging.

This, of course, sounds like heresy; and I readily admit that my own taste is conditioned to appreciate, in my Sherry, the faintly bitter taste that wine acquires from aging in oak. But how did wood come to be used for wine storage in the first place? The original wine containers of the ancients were earthenware jars called amphorae, with pointed bases which were stuck into the earth to hold them upright. Wood came into use much later, as a substitute capable of being built to hold larger quantities for mass production.

But now there is stainless steel, which does not cause wine to cloud as other metals do; and linings of glass and plastic are available for tanks made of concrete and metal. Germany has taken the lead in abandoning wood, and Rhine wines fermented and matured entirely in stainless-steel and glass-lined tanks are already being found superior to those aged in oak. American vintners are silently following; and I even know of one winery which has lined its wooden tanks with plastic in order to protect its wine from wood.

Another example of the technology revolution is the declining use of corks. Ever since the advent of easily-removed screw caps for bottles it has been contended that only a cork, made from the bark of cork oak trees in Spain and Portugal, can furnish a satisfactory closure for wine. Asked why, the vintner has usually replied that the cork allows the aging wine to "breathe." Here he has contradicted himself, of course, since contact with air is one of the major things from which vintners try to protect all of their wines except the Sherries and similar types, which are deliberately encouraged to oxidize, thus developing some of their "nutty" flavor. As yet nobody has furnished any proof that corks seal wines any more efficiently than screw caps do, or that aging in the bottle proceeds at a better rate with one type of closure than with the other.

In recent years some Champagne producers have abandoned the use of corks in favor of similarly shaped plastic plugs. Although these plugs are easily removed, they can leak if the insides of bottle necks vary in diameter, and when they do, the result is flat Champagne.

Why is it that virtually all of the higher-priced nonsparkling wines still come sealed with long, straight corks —which cost extra—not with screw caps? The answer, apparently, is a combination of tradition, consumer psychology, and the fact that vintners are not yet convinced that caps won't corrode or work loose during long periods of aging. Besides, there is no question that a corked bottle is better looking, and the ceremony of drawing the cork (if it comes out, that is) imparts an indefinable something to the occasion.

Lastly, let us discuss another puzzling subject about which wineries are not talking—wine bottles.

Why must Burgundy types, both white and red, come only in the narrow-shouldered, broad-based bottles which distinguish these particular wines? Why the broad-shouldered, narrower-waisted Claret shape, the tall, slender Hock bottle, the straight-necked one for Sherry, or the bulbous-necked one for Port?

The answer, so far as these shapes—completely meaningless to the average consumer—are concerned, is that they are solely a matter of tradition. The same tradition, if honored completely, would require the British to drink their wines from the original bottle of their history; it was made of leather.

There are, nevertheless, two characteristics of traditional bottles which have served useful purposes. One is the "push-up" in the base of some bottles. Although some believe that this device was originally intended to make the container seem larger than it really is, there is no doubt that in the early days, when most wines contained sediment, the sediment tended to form at the bottom, around the "push-up."

The other valuable aspect of the traditional bottles is their color.

Europe's old-time vintners learned long ago that sunlight injures the flavor of wine. That is why they use dark-colored bottles. But many American wineries have preferred to put their products in clear glass which lets the consumer see what he is buying. Recently, however, vintners with a college education have discovered that the sun's ultraviolet rays can spoil the taste of delicate wines, and also that these rays destroy certain vitamins in the wine. The newer trend, therefore, is again toward bottle colors which filter out ultraviolet light.

I am happy to report that this matter of light protection has not revived the post-prohibition attempt to popularize wine in cans. For I am not one of those who would strip wine of all its romantic atmosphere.

CHAPTER 10

SOME LABELS UNRIDDLED

IF THE VINTNERS OF THE WORLD HAD united in a mischievous effort to confuse the buyers of their products, they could scarcely have succeeded better than they have done without even trying. Surely there is no other widely used food or beverage whose bottles, cans, or boxes display more confusing information and less actual guidance to the average occasional consumer than the labels on wine bottles do.

In the earlier chapter entitled "Wine Unraveled," I shuffled the principal types of wine available in North America and grouped them roughly according to how they might taste. Now I shall try to unriddle some of the mystifying type names, flavor terms, alcohol contents, medals, estates, *crus,* grape names, and what—if anything—geographic designations mean.

HOW DRY IS "DRY"?

Let me start with seven words vintners use to describe degrees of product sweetness: "dry," "*sec,*" "*brut,*" "*na-*

ture," "*doux*," "cream," and "*haut*." Here we have an example of what semanticist S. I. Hayakawa, the author of *Language in Action*, meant when he wrote: "The writer of a dictionary is a historian, not a lawgiver." Dictionaries, Hayakawa contends, merely record what words have meant in the distant or immediate past—not what they mean today. For only one of the seven terms supposed to designate degrees of wine sweetness actually means what it says.

If the following explanation happens to inspire some hilarity, please remember that it is intended to be purely serious and factual.

There can be little doubt that the original Sherries and Champagnes—generations ago—were sweet. But it seems that certain high-placed connoisseurs in England objected to the sweet taste, demanded wines made dry, and were accommodated with "dry" Sherry and "*sec*" Champagne. ("Dry" meant non-sweet; "*sec*" meant the same in French.)

Soon—as the story goes—the wine snobs of that era, noting that people with prestige as connoisseurs drank only the "dry" and "*sec*" wines, began insisting on having their wines so labeled, too. But most people, then as now, prefer wines that taste sweet; and the vintners of that early era soon discovered the way to prosperity. They simply made the wines sweet but labeled them dry.

When the connoisseurs began to complain that their "dry" and "*sec*" wines were no longer dry, the vintners again obliged—by finding new words for the labels. They came up with "extra dry" for genuinely dry Sherry, and unsweetened Champagne became "*brut*" (French for "rough," "raw," or "unadulterated").

But soon the cycle was repeated: fashion-conscious Britons demanded wines with the "extra-dry" and "*brut*" labels—and these gradually became sweet, too. So now we have "bone-dry" Sherries and "*nature*" Champagne—while "dry," "extra dry," "*sec,*" and "*brut*" wines are gradually becoming sweeter.

How long it will be before the snobs prevail once more —and vintners will need to find still more words that mean non-sweet—is anybody's guess.

Meanwhile, many Americans are saying: "I only like wines that are dry," imagining that the word means "high quality." Of course they are only fooling themselves, because when they do taste a dry wine, they complain that it tastes "sour." (A really sour wine is a spoiled wine; it has refermented, forming acetic acid and turning into vinegar.)

Moreover, the rape of "dry" as a descriptive term for beverages is now complete, because a "dry" Martini cocktail has come to mean only that the once-mandatory ingredient—Vermouth—is now administered with an atomizer; and most of today's Martini drinkers are sipping virtually straight gin.

I said there is one wine-sweetness term which actually means what it says. That is "*doux,*" which means "sweet" in French. French Champagne producers did once sell a little of this honestly labeled product in Russia, but they find little sale for it in the United States. In this country, perhaps because of the national concern over calories, "sweet" in any language somehow seems to be a naughty word. Consequently, an extra-sweet Champagne, in order to sell to Americans, has to be labeled—of all things—"*demi-sec*" or "semi-dry."

This is also why the sweetest Sherries are labeled "Cream Sherry."

The demand for wines with "dry" labels even fools some vintners. They make truly dry wines and never quite understand why their sales are so disappointing.

At any rate, you can be assured from the foregoing paragraphs that "bone-dry" Sherries and "*nature*" Champagnes are likely to be quite dry—at least for the time being—and that "cream" Sherries and "*demi-sec*" and "*doux*" Champagnes will surely be very sweet. As for the rest, while you know that "dry" is theoretically sweeter than "extra dry" and that "*sec*" should be sweeter than "*brut*," you cannot be sure of how dry or sweet the individual wine so designated will be, until you first learn what the individual vintner means by his label.

This brings us to the strange story of "Haut Sauterne."

In France, where Sauternes originated around the Bordeaux village of that name, this type of white wine is always semi-sweet. In America, most Sauterne is quite dry. In order to supply a Sauterne as sweet as the French—but to avoid labeling it sweet—American vintners have adopted another French term. They call it "Haut Sauterne."

But while visiting in France a few years ago I was told emphatically there is no such French wine as "Haut Sauterne." And I recently received a letter from the Institut National des Appellations d'Origine des Vins et Eaux-de-Vie, repeating that denial. It reads, in part:

"Concerning Haut-Sauterne, we have no idea how it came to be used. There is no such name in France, only Sauternes, name of a village and of a wine produced in the delimited area around this village. Haut means high. It is used in geography to designate part of a village or region higher than the other one. . . ."

What adds to the mystery is that I know for a fact that French vintners do ship to the United States wines labeled "Haut Sauternes." I have seen the bottles.

Be that as it may, the French pronunciation of "*haut*" is, of course, "oh," as in O'Leary or O'Reilly. Most Americans, however, including the vintners who make "Haut Sauterne," pronounce it "hot."

This might account for an experience reported to me recently by my late Sausalito neighbor, author Eugene Burns.

Burns and his wife were flying home from the Orient on a Japanese airliner. It was Christmas Eve. When time came for dinner on the plane, the kimono-clad stewardesses brought out a surprise for the passengers. It was a complete holiday dinner, including turkey and all the trimmings. With it they served glasses of Sauterne—piping "Haut"!

Right here is as good a point as any to explain still

another puzzling term you find on some American Sauterne labels: "chateau."

This one began about a century ago, when the only way California vintners could sell their wines in eastern markets was to put counterfeit French labels on them. One such widely imitated label was that of the most famous of all French Sauternes, the Château d'Yquem.

As the years passed, California wines gradually achieved recognition for quality in their own right, and the California wine acquired a somewhat more informative label as "*California* Chateau Yquem."

But following the repeal of prohibition the United States Government summarily outlawed the use of all foreign proprietary names on American wines, and "Yquem" was the principal casualty.

What did the California vintners do? Deprived of "Yquem," they preserved "chateau." So now, when you see "chateau" on a California wine label, immediately preceding the name of the vineyard, it does not refer to anybody's feudal castle. All it means is that the wine in the bottle is an extra-sweet California Sauterne.

This whole semantical nightmare about sweetness was climaxed with a paradox during the 1940's, when the so-called "kosher" Concord grape wines appeared on the national scene. For these products are made syrupy sweet by massive additions of sugar. Here the United States Government was faced with a problem, because the quantity of sugar the "kosher" producers used was more than the federal regulations allowed any wine to contain, unless it was called "imitation."

The Government decided to permit their sale, but in order to warn the public, decreed that each label must contain the following phrase in capital letters: SWEETENED WITH EXCESS SUGAR.

But to the amazement of all concerned the public, instead of being warned not to buy, welcomed the promise of extra-sweet wines, and bought them freely—apparently not caring whether the sugar came from grapes, cane, beets, or corn, as long as it was there. In fact the EXCESS SUGAR phrase helped to make the kosher producers millionaires almost overnight. As they used to say about a certain controversial pianist who was derided by experts for "hamming" the classics, these winemakers cried all the way to the bank.

Finally the Government gave up and dispensed with the "excess sugar" requirement; and the labels now merely read: "specially sweetened."

The kosher-type wines are not the only ones containing added sugar. All fruit wines—such as the blackberry, loganberry, and apple types—are similarly sweetened. Also, the grapes grown in eastern and midwestern states and Canada do not develop sufficient natural grape sugar to ferment into standard wines, and consequently they require a moderate supplement of non-grape sugar.

California, however, has long had a vintner-sponsored state regulation prohibiting the addition of sugar to its traditional wine types—and at last reports the state's vintners were not entirely happy about it, because they have discovered that when wines do need sweetening for any reason, sugar gives them better flavor than grape syrup does.

Some of the European countries, too, prohibit adding sugar to wine, or require that the labels show that the wines are sugared. But while it is well known that many European wines (especially French Burgundies and German Rhine wines) are thus sweetened, I have yet to see a single label that admitted it.

This raises the question of what is meant by the legend that appears on millions of wine bottles, proclaiming their contents are "100 per cent pure." Since sugared wines are as eligible as any to claim purity, the phrase seems quite meaningless; and I have heard some vintners express the wish that they had never begun using it. It assuredly does *not* mean that the wines without the "pure" label are in any respect impure.

WHAT ALCOHOLIC CONTENTS MEAN

Historically, some of the earliest pure-food laws were aimed at stopping the adulteration of wines, because synthetic versions of the product have been sold in many countries during periods of grape scarcity. The cardinal, most ancient sin—that of watering wines to stretch their volume—has been stopped, however, at least in the United States, by the federal regulation which requires every bottle to state its alcoholic content. When government inspectors find a wine containing less alcohol than the label states, they have a made-to-order case against the offending bottler.

In table wines (sometimes called "light," "natural," or "dinner" wines) the alcohol is created entirely by the natural fermentation of sugars, and rarely exceeds 14 per cent of the wine's volume. The dessert wines, on the other hand, contain brandy (pure wine spirits, distilled from wine), which is added to arrest fermentation before the sugars have completely fermented—thus keeping these wines sweet. Most dessert-wine labels give the alcoholic content as 20 per cent.

However, these figures do not give the exact strength. Because grapes, yeasts, and wines are temperamental, government regulations permit table wines to vary over a range of three percentage degrees, so that "Alcohol 12 per cent by Volume" on a label can mean that the contents of the bottle actually test as low as 10½ per cent or as high as 13½ per cent. A leeway of two degrees is permitted on dessert wines, so that "20 per cent" really means 19 to 21 per cent.

You never see labels with figures above 21 per cent, for a very good reason: When a wine exceeds that level, the federal tax suddenly is more than tripled.

In fact, this matter of tax rates helps to explain why the wine "class" names are so confusing—why, for example, the extremely sweet kosher type is nevertheless called a "table" wine, and why Dry Sherry—although primarily an appetizer wine—is nevertheless lumped with the sweet "dessert" wines.

The reason is that the Federal Government taxes the standard nonsparkling wine types at two different rates, depending on their alcoholic content. (The rates in 1964 were 17 cents per gallon on wines not exceeding 14 per cent, and 67 cents per gallon on those between 14 per cent and 21 per cent.) Since there are thus two distinct tax classes, each class had to have a name. For many years the Government called the first group "light wine" and the stronger group "fortified wine." But the industry detested the word "fortified," which gave the public the unfortunate impression that the stronger wines were being purposely spiked to make them more intoxicating. Finally the Government was persuaded to rename the groups for the principal uses to which most of the wines are put. Hence, "table wine" and "dessert wine."

But, people keep asking, why do the alcoholic content figures on the bottles vary so? Why do some Port and Sherry labels say 20 per cent, others 18 per cent, and still others (in a few parts of the nation) read only 16 per cent?

Let me first explain the conundrum of the 16 per cent Port and Sherry. Certain states impose local restrictions or special taxes on full-strength dessert wines. Their peculiar laws led, following the repeal of prohibition, to the creation of low-alcohol wines resembling Port, Sherry, and other standard dessert wines. The Government allowed these confusing variations to be labeled "Light Port" and "Light Sherry." Most vintners wish that these strange labels had never come into existence.

The other variations in the strength of Port and Sherry result mainly from an honest disagreement between California wine men and those of other states and nations over what minimum alcoholic content is needed to keep a dessert wine sound during the rigors of shipment. The Federal Government decided that 17 per cent is enough alcohol for Sherry, and 18 per cent for Port. But California accepted the view of its vintners, and set its legal minimum for Sherry and all other "dessert" wines at 19.5 per cent. (The print on California labels normally reads "20 per cent.")

Table wines' alcoholic contents vary, too, depending on the sugar content of their grapes. Grapes as sweet as 28 degrees Brix (the scale by which winemakers measure sugar content) can ferment—when completely dry—to about 15 per cent alcohol. Grapes of 18 Brix can produce about 9 per cent. California, where fully-mature grapes are the rule, enforces a minimum of 10 per cent alcohol for its white table wines and 10½ per cent for its reds; but the Federal Government allows wines as low as 7 per cent. Thus, while most table wines you find in stores are well above the California minimums, you often find wines from Germany, where the grapes are seldom very sweet, and sometimes from Bordeaux, labeled as containing 9 per cent or even less alcohol.

You can expect some of the California minimums to be reduced in years to come. Especially that state's vintners are beginning to notice that those 9 per cent German white wines not only have excellent keeping quality, but that some of their delicate flavor stems from their low alcoholic content.

How do wines compare in strength with other alcoholic beverages? Beer, of course, is the lowest, ranging usually from 4 per cent to 5 per cent by volume. Ales are usually stronger, ranging from 4.7 to as high as 8 per cent. Hard cider, the homemade kind, reaches about 7 per cent.

Sake, the Japanese rice brew (a beverage that is traditionally served hot), is usually around 16 per cent, and is classed by the United States Government as "wine" for labeling purposes and as "beer" for tax purposes.

Vermouths are flavored wines, and vary from 16 per cent to 20 per cent.

But all of the stronger beverages measure their alcohol in "proof spirits," a term which in the United States is simply double the actual per cent alcoholic content by volume of the drink. So divide each of the following "proof" figures in half to calculate the alcohol by volume: Cordials or liqueurs, 52 to 110 proof. Gins, 80 to 94 proof. Rums, 80 to 151 proof. Vodkas, whiskies, and brandies, 80 to 100 proof. A "bottled in bond" whisky or brandy is always at least 100 proof; that is, 50 per cent alcohol.

WHY WINE NAMES ARE CONFUSING

Nothing on a wine label can possibly confuse the public as completely as the names of the wines themselves do. The nomenclature tangle is so complete that I am certain no person lives who could describe the tastes and colors represented by all of the wine names popular in various parts of the world.

It is easier to explain how the tangle came about than it is to untwist it. The reason is that all winemaking in North and South America (Australia and South Africa might as well be mentioned here, too) began as an art imported from Europe.

With the art came the language of wine. And the language of wine types in Europe—as in the ancient Near East, where wine was born—is mainly a language of geography, not of flavor. In other words, most kinds of wine produced in Europe are named for the places where they are grown.

Thus, Sauternes began around the village of that name in Bordeaux; Burgundy and Champagne originated in the French regions so named; Port was named by the British for the City of Oporto in Portugal, and Sherry is a word the British coined because they could not pronounce the name of the Spanish town from which the wine came—Jerez de la Frontera (originally spelled Xeres).

These names, and many others of origins mainly geographical, spread throughout the civilized world long ago on the labels of the wines. The words became part of other languages. France and Germany adopted Port and Sherry. Spanish vintners began making Burgundy and Rhine wine, and the European winemakers who emigrated to the New World faithfully named their new wines for their former homelands.

Eventually, the European vintners realized that their treasured wine names were no longer exclusively their own. Alarmed, they demanded that the use of all geographical wine names be restricted to wines produced in the districts the words originally represented. Their governments obliged by entering into international treaties. Spain, Portugal, France, Germany, and other nations signed such agreements. Great Britain also obliged, despite loud protests from the young wine industries of Australia and South Africa.

But Europe had awakened too late to win back its names from America. European wine types had become permanent parts of the American language over a century ago—along with Russian rye bread, Swiss cheese, Danish pastry, and Dutch ovens.

For decades, and to this day, the French Government, in particular, has protested endlessly to the United States State Department, with little effect. French vintners bitterly complain that America not only has pirated French names, but even awards medals to vintners for using them!

The American wine industry's reply is that no imitation is intended—that every label clearly shows that the wine is American, not European—and that vintners here would prefer to use other names, if any existed in their language. Shall we stop calling our dishes china? they ask. Or order sports writers to cease reporting that the prize fighter's punch drew claret?

To placate the French, the United States Government requires American labels to use large type in printing the American place of origin on labels, in direct conjunction with any wine-type name of foreign origin. Labels say "California Burgundy," "American Sherry," "Ohio Port," "New York State Champagne," et cetera. Further, only a few of these wine-type names are allowed, and all foreign proprietary names (such as Château d'Yquem) are forbidden.

According to my latest letter from Paris, the French are now hopeful of persuading Chile to revise the language of its wines. But thus far France has made no progress whatever in protesting the "Sovietsky Champagne" produced in Russia.

WHAT GRAPE NAMES MEAN

At this juncture the American wine snob enters the controversy. He displays his erudition by condemning United States wines as "imitations," simply because of the international type names they bear.

Weary of defending themselves, many winemakers, primarily those producing higher-priced wines, have turned to a relatively new kind of label. They now name each wine for the grape variety from which it is made. So now we have names such as White Pinot, Pinot Blanc, Red Pinot, Pinot Noir, and Pinot Chardonnay to perplex the public; also Sauvignon Blanc, Green Hungarian, Chenin Blanc, Gamay, Grignolino, Semillon, Traminer, Elvira, Niagara, Charbono, Sylvaner—to name a few of these delicious impedimenta to public understanding of wine.

If you cannot spell or pronounce these names, and cannot tell varietally labeled wines apart by tasting them, do not let it trouble you. I assure you that very few people who are not professional experts (and not many of the latter) can actually distinguish, by tasting a white wine, whether it is made of Semillon, Sylvaner, Riesling, or Chardonnay grapes. And the average official wine judge will admit his inability, if you administer truth serum (or enough of his favorite wine), to tell Cabernet Sauvignon from Gamay or from Pinot Noir. On the occasions when I happen to guess these wines right in blind tastings, I always swell with pride and brag to my family about my achievement.

Dame Nature being true to her capricious self, there are far too many varieties, and variations within varieties, with only faint differences in flavor. For example, there are at least three kinds of Cabernet: Cabernet Sauvignon, Cabernet Franc, and Ruby Cabernet. There are many departures from Gamay Beaujolais, and numerous strains of Pinot Noir.

Meanwhile, in the University of California's vineyard at Davis a remarkable young professor named Harold P. Olmo had been busily engaged for several years in marrying old grape varieties to create brand new ones. He has already introduced several, including Emerald Riesling and Ruby Cabernet—whose names you now see on wine labels—and is testing more that also show promise.

Mistaken identification of grapes contributes to the maze. Many growers (in Europe as well as in America) do not know the right names of their vines. And it is an open secret that when Agoston Haraszthy, the Hungarian nobleman who is called the father of modern California viticulture, imported 100,000 cuttings of European vines to his adopted state in 1862, the labels on many of the 1,400 varieties became hopelessly mixed. Recently a vintner who had won many customers for his excellent Traminer wine was horrified to learn from the University that the grapes in his vineyard were not Traminer at all, but a little-known variety called Red Veltliner.

Besides, you may as well know that the average varietal wine is not made entirely of the grape whose name it bears. Because wines need blending to achieve flavor balance, the regulations permit blending with as much as 49 per cent of other varieties. And although the Government says the flavor of the variety on the label must predominate, you sometimes find a cut-priced varietal in which the 49 per cent overpowers the 51 per cent.

However, not all grape variety names for wines are necessarily confusing. A few of them have conveyed unmistakable color and flavor meanings for generations. Muscatel, for example, is recognized by almost everyone who has ever tasted it as an amber or golden sweet wine with the powerful flavor of Muscat grapes. "Muscat," however, is often deceptive; wines so labeled may be either sweet or dry. Zinfandel, a grape of somewhat mysterious origin, gives its name to a popular California Claret, in which—if your nose is remarkably sensitive—you sometimes can detect the faintly raspberry-like flavor of this variety. Longfellow sang the praises of Catawba, a white wine (there is also a sparkling version) made from that Labrusca grape, principally in Ohio. Vintners who make their Rosé wines of Grenache grapes like to add that grape name to their Rosé labels. And when you mention "grape flavor" to most Americans, they automatically think of a single grape—the Concord variety—which provides the taste of the kosher-wine type and of most fresh and frozen grape juices.

In the foregoing list I might also mention Riesling, which long ago became so popular as a synonym for Rhine wine (a type best made from the White Riesling variety) that American vintners once tried to persuade the Government that Riesling no longer meant any particular grape. (The Government was not persuaded.)

Lest my frank explanations be taken to imply that I do not like varietals, let me add that I regularly buy them. One reason is that many vintners nowadays use varietal labels for the very choicest of their wines. Another is that, being an oenophile, I find special enjoyment in detecting each grape's personality in a wine. And besides, I like to drink as many different wines as possible with my dinners.

WHAT GEOGRAPHY REALLY MEANS

Returning to Europe's geographical labeling, while place names do not mean everything, as the Europeans claim they do, they do mean something. The climate of Bordeaux is kind to the grape varieties that make red and white Bordeaux wines, and each delimited district within the Bordeaux area has found, by centuries of experience, which grapes thrive best within its borders. Burgundy nurtures the Pinots, Gamays, and Melons best; the Rhone Valley favors the Petit Sirah; Germany's Rhineland makes its best wines from White Riesling. As a result, the European geographic names have—to some extent—a certain varietal significance.

The flavorful grapes grown in the famed French districts produce only poor wines when planted in southern France, the source of most French wines. There, consequently, undistinguished, heavy-bearing varieties are cultivated, and the southern French wines are so neutral that vast quantities of good wine are imported in tank ships from Algeria and Tunisia for blending. The wine the average Frenchman drinks is a blend of poor French wine and better wine from across the Mediterranean.

It is mainly climate that governs a district's ability to grow the superior grapes successfully. The Europeans believe that soil composition is equally important, but modern research questions whether any chemicals in the earth actually enter the flavor of a wine. Yet some soils, such as the gravelly kinds, do hold the sun's heat better than others do, and help grapes to mature.

It might interest the French to know that California, too, is jealous of its name, and that the same applies to individual California localities.

For example, when a California vintner ships 16 per cent "Light Sherry" to a state which discriminates against the genuine article, he must have special permission from the California Department of Public Health. And in so doing he loses the right to label such wine with the name of California; it may only be called "American" Light Sherry. And while a "New York State" or "Ohio" wine may contain as much as 25 per cent of wine made elsewhere (and many of them are blends with wine or grape syrup from California), no wine can claim to be Californian unless it is made 100 per cent from California grapes in California.

Equally jealous of their names are the leading California table-wine districts. The Livermore Valley is noted for its outstanding Sauterne types, and its vintners show their district's name on their labels. Napa Valley's name on a label automatically commands higher prices for its table wines, red and white. Sonoma, Santa Clara, Santa Cruz, and Mendocino are all known to connoisseurs for their distinctive table wines. The Cucamonga district in southern California and the Lodi district in the Central Valley have borrowed a leaf from the French practice, and have persuaded the United States Government to recognize specific geographical limits of their viticultural areas for labeling purposes.

The University of California has measured the average annual hours of sunshine in each of the state's vineyard areas, and recommends specific grape varieties that grow best in each locality. This has furnished the scientific explanation of why the state's warm valleys produce the best dessert wines, but why most experts look for their finest table wines in the cooler coastal counties.

Elsewhere in the Americas districts' climates determine where grapes are grown and how they taste. In the United States, New York's Finger Lakes district is noted for Champagne and other distinctively flavored wines, and the Sandusky-Lake Erie Islands and Cincinnati districts of Ohio have won fame for their special types. Other winegrowing districts are Washington's Puget Sound and Yakima Valley areas, Oregon's Willamette Valley, the Council Bluffs region in Iowa, the Missouri River vineyards of Missouri, all of southwestern Michigan, portions of New Jersey, Virginia, North Carolina, and Arkansas. In all, wine is grown in twenty-seven states, and with the recent introduction of the hardy French hybrid grapevines by Philip Wagner of Baltimore, winegrowing is expected to spread to a number of other areas. Wagner's hybrids are reported becoming especially popular in the Niagara peninsula of Canada, already noted for a number of excellent wines.

The embattled French thus have some support for their argument that place names deserve protection. However, they should have started much earlier. So should the city of Boston, whose chefs are quoted as objecting in vain to the designation of beans, prepared by inexpert cooks in other parts of the nation, as "Boston baked beans."

There is still another side to this entire subject of district nomenclature. The ancient wine-laden oxcart is still seen in some of Europe's wine lands, but tank motor trucks are appearing on the same roads with increasing frequency. In both France and Italy, but especially in America, we see the growth of large wineries which bring wines from different grape districts to their central cellars for blending and sale under the brands they advertise. Does the spread of swift modern transportation mean that the era of geographic wine labeling is approaching an end?

Obviously France does not think so. The French since 1935 have been tightening the laws which define the borders of their viticultural districts, large and small. More and more you see on French wine labels the words "*Appellation Contrôlée,*" which are supposed to mean that the contents of the bottle were grown in the delimited district whose name it bears, from approved grape varieties only, and according to the locally recognized method of vinification. Yet there is no one country that imports more wine in bulk for blending with its own production than France does, and the French are known to be better at writing strict laws than at enforcing them.

Apparently long-suffering Europe has ceased complaining about our tendency to anglicize its wine types. At any rate, the Bordeaux producers have not expressed themselves recently about American vintners' omission of the final "s" in the name of Sauternes. But some United States producers take the matter seriously, and their labels always contain the ninth letter, which makes people wonder whether the bottle's contents are plural. Perhaps the Old World feels as Mark Twain did when he said he had no respect for anyone who knows only one way to spell a given word.

From the average wine shopper's standpoint, American vintners' use of Old World names sometimes makes better sense than the European labels do.

For example, United States wineries have grown weary of labeling red sparkling wine "Sparkling Burgundy" while the white sparkling type is Champagne. Now, by obtaining a simple change in federal regulations, they have made "Sparkling Burgundy" synonymous with a new term: Red Champagne.

Another case is American Ports, all of which are at least sweet. But the Portuguese confuse the Port name by also selling "dry" Port and a "Muscatel" Port. Still another is American Tokay (in no way related to the grape of that name), a medium-sweet tawny-pink dessert wine. The name has much clearer meaning than the original Hungarian (spelled Tokaj), which can signify wines either red or white, dry or sweet, or in between.

The job of simplification is far from finished, however. To drive the average vintner wild, ask him to tell you the flavor difference among America's Rhine wine, Chablis, and Dry Sauterne—or between Claret and Burgundy. In general, there isn't any.

THE NEW WINE NAMES

As though the thousands of old wine-type names were not enough, a flood of entirely new ones hit the national market beginning in 1956. United States vintners had suddenly gotten busy creating entirely new wine types, with added non-grape flavors designed to please the iced-Cola-and-apple-pie tastes of modern Americans. Most of these products are identified by words like "apéritif wine" and "grape wine with natural pure flavors." But the coined names they bear, referring to birds, animals, and to anything but grapes or wine, resemble nothing ever before seen on a wine label anywhere. If their overnight success is any indication of the future, these new products may well remodel all old concepts of what constitutes wine.

OTHER LABEL MYSTERIES EXPLAINED

One kind of legend on wine labels that especially puzzles shoppers is the group of words supposedly describing variations within a single wine type. The varying sweetnesses of Sherries and Champagnes, already explained, are one example. Another is the sub-types of Port.

White Port is easily distinguished from the red, of course. But then we have "Tawny" and "Ruby" Ports as well as the traditional type with no qualifying term. Most Tawny Ports are what the word implies: tawny in color, presumably from long aging in the cask; but they also sometimes are slightly less sweet than the other subtypes. Ruby Port is sometimes sweeter than the others, and is as rich and colorful as its name implies.

The Germans offer an interesting series of qualifying terms for their Rhine wines. A wine labeled *Auslese* supposedly means that the grapes were fully ripe and carefully selected. *Beerenauslese* is a claim that each individual grape berry was carefully selected as perfectly ripe. *Spätlese* signifies that the grapes were left on the vine to become partly raisined and to grow the "noble mold" of French Sauternes. *Trockenbeerenauslese* means the same as *Spätlese,* except that the grapes are almost completely raisined. The latter wine is correspondingly very sweet and enormously expensive.

Another German term has charmed many American buyers because of its literal translation. It is Liebfraumilch, which means "milk of the Blessed Virgin." All it actually tells you, however, is that it is just another German Rhine wine, and not necessarily from the most distinguished vineyards. Few of them deign to use the word.

Most confusing among European label designations are the "first," "second," "third," "fourth," and "fifth" *crus* (growths) on the labels of leading Bordeaux vineyards. They represent a classification of the region's most famous estates, ranking each in the order of the quality of its wines. The classification was made in 1855.

Although many of the châteaux have changed hands and replanted their vineyards during a century, a review of these rankings in 1955 produced no changes whatever. Thus—as any book about Bordeaux wines will tell you—many a third or fourth *cru* is conceded to be superior to many a first and second *cru*.

Producers of California's Rosés are providing some puzzles, too. Some vintners offer two versions of this pink wine—one called "Vin Rosé" and the other simply "Rosé." One is sweet, one is dry—but, as noted in Chapter 3, different producers use the terms with opposite meanings. Besides, the puzzling word *vin* is merely French for "wine."

"Solera" on some of the Sherry labels arouses some curiosity, which is usually answered by explanations on the bottles' back labels. It refers to the Spanish method of fractional blending—an intricate system of aging wines gradually in batteries of small casks, periodically mixing portions of new wine with old.

A number of rather ordinary-sounding words have special meanings on bottles of wine, and vintners have been known to battle at lengthy public hearings for the right to use them. The public may not notice, for example, that some labels say the wine was "produced and bottled by" a given person, vineyard, or company, while other wineries say "made" instead of "produced," and still other wines simply read: "bottled by . . ."

The significance of "produced" is that the vintner named must have crushed, fermented, matured, and bottled at least 75 per cent of the wine in the bottle. Large wineries, however, often exchange wines with one another to maintain balanced inventories and regularly contract with other cellars to produce wines for them, and also buy some wines from bulk producers. So, rather than attempt to segregate for separate labeling the lots fermented in their own cellars, they usually compromise with labels saying "made" instead of "produced."

"Bottled at the winery" is another legend of restricted use, meaning much the same as "produced." But "estate bottled" is the rare designation permitted only for use by the small wine-growing estates. It means that 100 per cent of the grapes were grown in the owner's vineyard, and that every drop of the wine in the bottle was made in his own adjoining cellar.

The estate-bottling winery, catering exclusively to the connoisseur, usually makes its labels furnish a complete blueprint of every wine. It tells the grape variety and the year it was grown and fermented, names the European type the wine resembles, and—by words like "produced" and "estate bottled"—informs the buyer where all of these operations were performed.

Other label mysteries are simple, however, compared to the problem of identifying the producer of a wine when the bottle bears a fictitious trade name. Some of the best wineries play this game of hiding their identities. One well-known vintner during 1964 was bottling his wines under forty-one different names—his own and forty others. The bottles bearing his fictitious names were generally priced lower than those identified as his own. Because I happen to recognize them, I always buy the bottles bearing his aliases. In his case they are real bargains.

Although at first glance this practice may seem naughty, there are some good reasons for its existence. Certain store chains regularly contract with wineries and food packers to supply them with merchandise under the chains' private brands. A winery which supplies such a chain may prefer not to be identified. The fictitious trade name is the solution.

There is also the vintner's problem of disposing of that part of his production which is not quite up to his top-quality standard. By selling his second-grade wine under a different name, he avoids injuring his reputation for high quality. This practice, by encouraging the bottling of wine at the winery where it is produced, is better from the consumer's standpoint than the alternative of letting it be shipped somewhere else for bottling.

If you insist on identifying the bottler of a wine bearing a winery name you never heard of, there is one way to get the information. Ask the nearest office of the United States Internal Revenue Service's Alcohol and Tobacco Tax Division. It may take a while to get an answer, however, because while there are in the United States approximately four hundred and forty-four bonded wine cellars and one hundred and three tax-paid wine-bottling houses, there probably are at least as many additional fictitious names on bottles of American wines.

TRUTH ABOUT MEDALS

Another thing you often find on labels is the story of how many medals the wine has won in assorted fairs and international expositions. This subject is good for an argument any time you can get two wine men together. Having twice been a wine judge at the California State Fair—sniffing scores of entries daily, swishing each around my tongue, conscientiously emptying my mouth to keep a clear palate for those to follow, and voting for the numbered samples I thought were best—I feel free to join the discussion.

I have no doubt that a wine which has won a gold, silver, or bronze medal in either the California State Fair or the Los Angeles County Fair—the two rival competitions held in California annually—is an excellent wine. This is true in spite of a certain difficulty—the problem of taste-blind judges.

I know one sincere fellow who, although he served on wine juries for many years, couldn't tell a Cabernet from sweet vino. Although he never realized it, his nerve endings were insensitive to certain flavors. The taste-blind judge problem was approaching solution, however, in 1957, when scores of candidates for judging assignments were first blind tested for tasting ability (I passed on that occasion), and again in 1958 (when I flunked).

But if you hope to rely on medal awards to guide you in buying wines you will most enjoy, you are likely to be disappointed, for several reasons.

For one thing, the California judges cannot award the gold medal to a wine simply because it is the most delicious wine competing. Instead, judges must search for faults in the wine—including technical faults most consumers could never detect—and finally measure the wine by its conformance to a set of rigid type specifications of color, acidity, astringency, and grape variety flavor. Often the one wine which would give you the most taste pleasure is thus ineligible for even an honorable mention.

For another, the sample which wins the medal represents a limited quantity of wine in the vintner's cellar; the medal is awarded only on the number of gallons in that lot. So, if you go to the store in your neighborhood to buy a medal-winning wine, your chance of getting the very same beverage the judges approved is remote indeed. Connoisseurs who live in California have the best opportunity to buy the prize winners. Some of them go direct to the wineries and snap up whatever is available.

As for the labels picturing medals awarded to vintages decades ago, they mean only that the winery made fine wine at some time in the past. It probably has good quality now, but this requires proof today.

Moreover, if you merely recall Paris and the golden apple he awarded to Helen of Troy, you remember that any contest depending on human judges' preferences inspires hot controversies, if not open hostilities. So you need not be surprised at the accusations that some vintners enter special lots of wine in the fairs simply to win medals. Nor need you wonder that many of the leading producers refuse to enter all such competitions. Some never have entered. Others have won so many medals in years past that they have simply decided to retire from the lists, like the undefeated ex-champions of sports.

The mature philosophy of Europe offers a bit of contrast to the American fuss over medals. Usually, when wine judgings are held in the Old World, every wine entered gets a medal.

STRANGE STORY OF CHAMPAGNE

Omitting several dozen other kinds of label jargon that other books may explain, I have reserved for the last the remarkable story of sparkling-wine nomenclature.

In France, "Champagne" means a white wine of the delimited Champagne district, containing bubbles produced by a secondary fermentation of the wine within the bottle. This involves a lengthy, arduous, and costly process, because the secondary fermentation not only produces gas, but also deposits a fine sandlike sediment. To get rid of the sediment, the bottles must be shaken and turned daily for a period of months until the deposit slides into the bottle's neck. At that point the neck portion is frozen, the cork removed, the sediment disgorged, and the missing wine replaced with more Champagne and a *dosage* of sweetening.

In the United States, too, producers must ferment wine in the bottle if they wish to label it Champagne.

But back in 1910 a Frenchman named Eugene Charmat

invented a simpler and quicker process which has come into wide use throughout the world. This is the "closed *cuvée*" method, in which the secondary fermentation takes place in large glass-lined tanks, from which the wine is bottled under pressure, conveniently leaving the sediment behind.

But the bulk-fermented wine cannot be labeled Champagne as such. The French law calls it only *vin mousseux* (sparkling wine). The United States Government's regulation allows it to be labeled "*Sparkling Wine—American* (or local place of origin) *Champagne—Bulk Process,*" and specifies that the extra words be printed on the label in especially prominent letters.

With a more attractive label, you would expect bottle-fermented Champagnes to be made of finer wines and to cost more than the bulk-process kind. This is true of some brands, but there are low-priced bottle-fermented Champagnes, too. And here is an industry secret.

It is a fact—which all makers of bottle-fermented Champagne will hotly deny—that not even the most experienced taster could possibly detect, by eye, nose, or mouth, any difference between a bottle-fermented wine and the same wine made bubbly by the simpler process. (I feel compelled to add, thereby incurring the wrath of the users of both the foregoing processes, that the same taster would also fail to tell the difference if the bubbles were pumped into the wine by artificial carbonation, as in soda pop.)

The bulk-process vintners constantly clamor to have

the California State Fair judge their products together with the bottle-fermented Champagnes. The makers of the latter object, and, as of this writing, have still prevented a joint judging.

Anyhow, you should know that the real difference between Champagnes is not the process, but the quality of the grapes and still wines from which they are made and the care and aging the products receive.

But the strangest part of the story is about the rates United States railroads formerly charged for transporting bubbly wines. For years "Sparkling Wine—Champagne—Bulk Process" traveled at the same rate as "still" (non-sparkling) wines. But Champagne, without the cheapening extra words, paid double rates—and the bottle-fermenting producers filed no objection.

Thus, a bottle-fermented red or pink sparkling wine, if the label read "Sparkling Burgundy" or "Sparkling Rosé," paid the low rate; but if the producer chose to label the very same wines "Red Champagne" or "Pink Champagne," he paid double.

In 1956 the railroads appealed to the Interstate Commerce Commission to eliminate this difference, in a case involving something like a half-million dollars a year in freight charges. An I. C. C. examiner heard the appeal, and recommended it be denied. It was not until 1959 that the two rates were finally made the same.

I have just noticed that the title of this chapter is

"Some Labels Unriddled." At this point I am inclined to concede that the reader—if he would understand all of the world's leading wine labels—must be referred to far more complete volumes published by other authors, who have found it necessary to devote separate books to the wines of single nations, and in some cases to the wines of individual regions within those nations.

CHAPTER 11

YOU CAN MAKE IT YOUR HOBBY

LESS STRENUOUS THAN GOLF or gardening, better tasting than the backs of old postage stamps, and somewhat more fragrant than my other chief diversion—fishing—is the hobby of wine.

Few other avocations offer as many widely different kinds of pleasure. This one ranges from cultivating your own vineyard to making your own wine; you can tour the world's wine lands; build a wine cellar; collect old labels, fancy stemware; test your palate by tasting—or simply enjoy elbow bending at home.

Wine also blends with gastronomy. All the noted amateur chefs are equally wine hobbyists, because high cuisine demands wine both as a seasoning and as an accompaniment at the table.

As for literature, few kinds of reading offer more pleasure to the senses than recollections of memorable meals artfully blended with great vintages. Wine libraries contain the whole history of civilization.

The wine hobbyist experiences the subtler joys. He

sees in his glowing wine the sky over vineyard hillsides; he inhales from it the essence of the countryside; he savors its bouquet, admires it as a work of art, and lets it infuse sunshine into his veins.

Nothing in this book—which is written to unscramble wine for those Americans still unacquainted with the beverage of mature, temperate people—is intended to deprecate the higher arts of wine appreciation. My hope is that it will attract more genuine hobbyists to the subject, because unlike the overcrowding of my favorite fishing holes, the more devotees of wine, the merrier.

Let me first, therefore, expand the references made in earlier chapters to the aging of wines; for here is the principal delight in this entire sphere.

Although most of the world's wines reach their peak in quality early, and thereafter decline, certain red table wines, a very few whites, and a substantial proportion of the Sherries and dessert wines develop superlative quality with long years in their bottles. The extent of their improvement in glass—after their preliminary maturing in casks—can be likened to the difference between wood merely planed and the same wood sandpapered, or to the difference between a rosebud and the full-blown flower.

But the selection of such wines requires study. Many of the leading Bordeaux producers, once noted for the longevity of their wines—vintages famed for living a half-century or longer—have changed their output in recent years to lighter, earlier-maturing wines. Even the Napa Valley Cabernet Sauvignons, of which I have tasted magnificent examples that were nearly fifty years old, are being made lighter and earlier maturing now than formerly, by drawing the wine off the grape skins before fermentation is complete. One reason for this is the modern consumer's apparent liking for fresher-tasting, lighter-bodied wines than formerly. Another is that vintners have come to realize that merchants cannot afford to keep stocks many years before sale. The California premium producers usually store their wines in bins at the wineries for a few months to a year after bottling—just to take off the rough edges, they say. But binning is expensive in terms of space, handling, and waiting for the proceeds of sale. Only the householder can reasonably be expected to buy wines for the special purpose of aging in the bottle.

Your fun is in making the selection, buying by the case, opening a bottle from time to time and discovering the exact moment at which such a wine blooms, so to speak, with its maximum bouquet and mellow goodness.

An example of the heights to which this art of selection can develop was furnished to me one spring day by that California oenophile, Dr. Salvatore Pablo Lucia. We were visiting a few cellars in the Santa Clara Valley, sampling the newly fermented, still yeasty-tasting wines from the casks. Lucia asked one winemaker whether he had ever entered wines in the State Fair. The answer was negative. "Enter this one when it matures," said the doctor.

Two years later his advice was followed. The wine won a gold medal.

One of the diversions of the kings of old was to similarly

tour the vineyards, taste wines in the wood, and select those to be aged and bottled for their cellars. Today this is still being done by the brokers of Burgundy and Bordeaux. ("Broker," by the way, originated from the French *broquier,* who tapped or "broke" a cask to draw wine.)

Every wine ages differently; in fact, among very old ones each bottle is likely to be different. Venerable wines are temperamental, and should be handled gently. When carried for any distance or even shaken, they sometimes sulk for a time and need to rest before serving.

If you keep a table wine ten years or more, watch it, because some corks grow soft and shrink with age, and excess air gets into the bottle as wine evaporates. You can recork old wines after ten years or so, or reseal the bottle by removing the foil and dipping the bottle neck into melted sealing wax.

Note the advice in earlier chapters about sediment or crust, and especially about buying an efficient corkscrew.

All of this, of course, suggests having a home wine cellar. It need not be a vast vaulted cavern; the dark end of an apartment clothes closet can hold a dozen or more cases of wine. All that is necessary is to choose a cool spot that won't get too warm, yet won't freeze, where the temperature is as even as possible. While millionaires can afford air conditioning and temperature control, you can convert a spot in even a warm cellar by lining it with insulating wallboard.

Although in the past I have recommended building scalloped racks to fit individual bottles, I now favor one kind of storage arrangement above all others—diamond-shaped bins. These are simply constructed of parallel 1″ by 12″ boards. Lean them at a 45-degree angle between uprights, with short dividing pieces nailed 16″ apart to form the square compartments. Such bins hold the most wine in the least space, and the bottles don't roll about.

A cellar provides the opportunity to keep a cellar book. In it you can keep a record of your wines, of the foods you served them with, and how they tasted—a fascinating diary of pleasures. Some hobbyists keep label collections. One of my friends has all his guests autograph the label of a wine they have enjoyed, as a memento of a pleasant dinner.

Not only can you show off your cellar, but you can pay a guest a high compliment when he comes to dinner. Take him to the cellar and allow him the privilege of choosing the wine that is to be served. At the table, let him taste it first, and present him with the cork.

Your collection also solves many a gift problem. Few tokens of esteem for a friend are quite as personal as a bottle of rare wine. (Wine gifts, however, are mainly restricted to the state in which you reside. The strange laws of most states forbid shipments of even a single bottle from outside their borders. Ask the express company to name the few states to which it can make deliveries; alcoholic beverages are excluded from parcel post.)

Some hobbyists like to buy wines in large bottles, like the magnum (2/5 gallon), jeroboam (4/5 gallon), salmanazar (2½ gallons), and the nebuchadnezzar (4 gallons).

The foregoing capacities are only approximate. Most of these sizes, except the magnum (and the wicker-covered 4.9 gallon demijohn), are rarely obtainable in the United States. Wines age more slowly in these containers than in the popular "fifth"; and age more quickly in the half bottle or "tenth."

A wine collection enables you to hold truly great dinners, made so by their vinous accompaniment. Some gourmets write out the complete menus, or even have them printed, including the names of the guests in attendance.

You can also hold home or club wine tastings—a novel, temperate substitute for cocktail parties. These offer opportunities for special enjoyment, such as masking the bottles, distributing ballots on which guests vote their preferences on the wines by number on a simple score card—and finally unveiling the labels. I sometimes switch native and foreign wines between bottles, to observe how tastes are conditioned by labels.

In some cities, where laws permit, promotion-minded vintners have supplied wines without charge for clubs which sponsor tastings; and there are wineries in California where invitational tastings for connoisseurs are held from time to time.

A hobby in its own right is the cultivation of your own tasting ability. Taste, you know, is mostly smell. Your mouth can feel texture and temperature, but all your taste buds can record are sweetness, sourness, saltiness, and bitterness. (Hold your nose, close your eyes, and try to tell a raw potato from an apple or an onion.)

Each individual's taste differs from every other's. I, for example, find nothing objectionable in an excessively-sulphured Sauterne, while another individual cannot drink it; yet I am extremely sensitive to another wine defect (over-fining) which the next hundred people cannot even detect.

Test yourself as the professionals do, by pouring two similar wines into three numbered glasses, so that two of the glasses contain the same wine. Shuffle the glasses, and (without looking at the numbers) see if you can pick the glass containing the odd wine.

Wine tasting, *per se,* is best done before meals, because our sense of smell is keenest when we are hungry. In fact, researchers have found they can measure appetite by measuring olfactory acuity. Rinse your mouth or chew a bit of bread and rest a minute or two between wines. To be really sharp, avoid swallowing more than a few drops. True connoisseurs avoid strong drinks before dinner where fine wines are to be served; if they have any appetizer beverage, it is usually a dry Sherry or even a light white table wine.

Sweets also dull the palate. One day I accompanied an expert on a visit to a winery near Bordeaux. The wine-maker greeted us with a plate of confections. Later the expert told me: "That fellow tried a very old trick; he wanted to spoil our taste so that we wouldn't detect the defects in his wine."

An increasingly popular idea is the organization of small groups devoted to gourmet dining. The Cuisine Cousins, the one of which I am a member, consists of six couples who hold periodic "everybody-cook" dinners in one another's homes, at which everyone does his share of the food preparation. Our *chef-chef,* Kenneth Fry, does the food shopping. Then he distributes among us the recipes each is to prepare, together with the ingredients. By his advance planning we manage to get all the dishes prepared in the single kitchen. Another member is the *sommelier,* in charge of the wines. Still another, with artistic talents, creates an ornamental menu, which all of the members autograph as a treasured souvenir of the evening.

The Society of Medical Friends of Wine, founded at San Francisco in 1939, consists of physicians who are interested in the product's therapeutic values and also in gourmet dining with wine.

But the leading organization of wine hobbyists is the international Wine and Food Society, headquartered in London, which when I last counted had one hundred and one chapters in fourteen nations, including forty-three in the United States. Most of the American units have all-male memberships. All of us are disciples of President André L. Simon, a one-time journalist and Champagne salesman, who in 1905 published the first of his more than ninety books about wines and foods. Simon, by founding the Society in 1932, became the latter-day apostle of

Bacchus, Escoffier, and Brillat-Savarin in all of the English-speaking world.

Wine touring, too, has unlimited possibilities. A hospitable welcome awaits the hobbyist in most of the world's wineries, from California to Australia to Africa to Europe. In many cellars visitors are invited to taste; and wines always seem most delicious when sampled where they are grown. Moreover, almost anywhere you go you find that a vineyard district is also a gastronomic paradise.

Photography and painting blend especially with vineyard travel. Vintage scenes, ancient cellars, and the most beautiful of all fruits—the grape—have charmed artists since the beginning of time. And if you are fortunate enough someday to glimpse a vineyard in its full autumn dress of colors, you will never forget that brilliant sight.

But many other vinous diversions are available at home. A gourmet library is especially worth-while. One can keep abreast of viticultural progress through journals such as *Wines and Vines* (San Francisco), and with gastronomy in the pages of *Gourmet* (New York). I have seen marvelous collections of great menus, and have often thought of compiling a volume of historic toasts. (Toasting began, I have read, in ancient Greece, where guests poured a little wine into their hosts' glasses as a precaution against being poisoned. The custom got its name in the sixteenth century, when a bit of toasted bread was dropped into the wine when someone was to be honored.)

The history of wine is replete with odd and interesting facts. Kissing is said to have been invented by Roman husbands checking up on their bibulous wives. The first French Republic named a month *Vendemiaire* for the vintage season. The custom of christening a ship by breaking a bottle of Champagne on the bow at the launching presumably was a development from the human sacrifices once made to assure the benevolent protection of pagan gods. (Red wine came into use as a substitute for blood, but Champagne was later substituted because, being more expensive, it was held in higher esteem.) Superstitious sailors will tell you of "jinx" ships, christened with spring water during prohibition, which subsequently suffered mishaps or were wrecked.

Creating mixed drinks is a hobby of one of my doctor friends, who makes his own *apéritif* by adding a tablespoon of bitters to a bottle of light-bodied Port. Others have discovered that wines blend pleasantly with hard as well as soft drinks, and claim they can even make Bourbon whisky palatable by means of certain additions. (It is the Sweet Vermouth that does it in a Manhattan.)

The making of May wine provides an occasion for both a picnic and a traditional German or Viennese spring festival. You first go to the woods and search around the trunks of oaks for woodruff (German: Waldmeister), an herb bearing a white jessamine flower, with a perfume similar to new-mown hay. Bruise the leaves, add sugar or simple syrup, and any white wine—also orange juice if you like—and after various periods of steeping, you have an exceedingly fragrant drink.

The simplest recipes I have heard lately are for homemade Champagne. One friend makes his from white wine and ginger ale. Another simply carbonates Sauterne (with a little sugar added) in one of those glass pressure bottles that come with cartridges of carbon-dioxide gas. I have tasted the latter, and if the bubbles in the wine were longer lasting (which they could be if the wine were left overnight in the refrigerator), I would even recommend his recipe, for pure economy.

You can go all the way and make your own wine. This is legal and tax free, as long as you make no more than two hundred gallons, and first sign a form at the nearest office of the Federal Alcohol and Tobacco Tax Division. Here is a recipe from the University of California for homemade white wine:

"Use clean, freshly picked, sound ripe grapes of a juicy variety. . . . Crush with the hands or in a small kitchen-size screw-type fruit juice press. Place in two or three layers of cheesecloth over a large enamelware or aluminum pot. Never use zinc or galvanized pots or buckets. (*Avoid all contacts with metal.*) Gather up ends of cloth and press out juice with the hands, twisting cloth to get as much juice as possible. To each gallon of juice add ½ cake of compressed yeast, well broken up. Transfer to gallon jugs, or if there is enough juice, to a 5-gallon bottle, filling jugs or bottle only ¾ full. Place cotton in necks of jugs or bottles to exclude vinegar flies. Let ferment until fermentation ceases completely (no more bubbles, and taste of sugar entirely gone). Remove cotton and insert corks in bottles or jugs loosely, as some gas will form and might burst the containers during the next 10 or 12 days. When no more pressure forms, insert corks tightly. Let stand 2 more weeks. Pour off or siphon off into clean jugs or bottles, filling them nearly full. Cork. Let settle 4 to 5 weeks. Draw off. Bottle. Cork bottles. Set aside to age. Should be ready to use in 10 to 15 months."

But perhaps you prefer red wine. Here the University adds:

"Crush ripe, red wine grapes and remove stems. Place in stoneware jar, wooden tub, or small barrel with one head removed. Add ½ cake of well-broken-up fresh compressed yeast per gallon of crushed grapes. Stir three times a day during fermentation. Let ferment 5 days. Then strain and press as directed for white wine. Place in jugs. Plug with cotton. Let fermentation run to completion (no more gas). Then handle and age as directed for white wine."

Having tasted some samples made by methods like the foregoing, I scarcely feel like recommending the recipes. But perhaps I am difficult to please. It would be better to get the more complete recipes in the pamphlet *Wine Making at Home* by Professors Maynard Amerine and George Marsh, which makes it clear that the enemy—malignant bacilli—lurks at every stage of winemaking, and that absolute cleanliness (sulphuring your barrel, boiling your utensils, et cetera) is the salvation of those who venture to make wine.

Moreover, unless you use California wine-grape varieties, you must add sugar to the grapes; otherwise you will get a low-alcohol wine that will soon spoil. In fact, you ought first to measure your juice with a saccharometer, such as professional winemakers use, and never start fermentation until that instrument records at least 22 degrees.

Although I have bought wine in bulk and bottled it at home, I refuse to make my own. It would smell up my basement; the vintners do a better job, and their product is amazingly cheap.

If you want a completely absorbing hobby, do as George Washington did at Mount Vernon, Nicholas Longworth at Cincinnati, Ambassador James D. Zellerbach at Sonoma, and many other famous Americans have done, and as many are still doing today. That is, plant or buy your own vineyard. If you have both the patience to wait through long years and the finances to support an unprofitable endeavor you someday can serve your friends from bottles bearing your own name on their labels.

CHAPTER 12

HOW TO PERFUME YOUR COOKING

ALL OF THE BEST COOKBOOKS published in recent years contain numerous recipes calling for the use of wine. Yet it seems to me that some American cookbooks still tend to understate the case for this kitchen ingredient. Perhaps because the prohibitionist fringe among home economists might not approve, these authors fail to let their readers know that to be a truly great cook, one simply must use wine.

If you were to visit all of the famous chefs in hotels, restaurants, and clubs throughout the Western world, you would find wine in every one of their kitchens. Ask any of these masters of cuisine, and they will tell you that wines are indispensable ingredients of their art.

The reason for this is simple: Wine is an essential liquid seasoning; it accents and improves food flavors; and, in general, it perfumes your cooking.

You need no detailed recipe to prepare the mushroom soup you buy in a can. The directions say to add a can of water. Instead of only water, include a few spoonfuls of Sherry. Try it and you will see what I mean.

Frying an egg? Add a teaspoon of Sherry. Preparing spaghetti sauce? Don't leave out red wine. When you're serving strawberries, pour on a little Port.

All stews demand wine; roasts basted with it are subtly improved; even the humble hamburger takes on glamor from a few ounces of Burgundy in the skillet or baking dish.

As for sea food (the kind of cooking I, as an ardent fisherman, do oftenest), you need only be reminded that most fishes have odor like—well—fish. Add white table wine, or better yet, marinate a few hours or overnight in wine, and you discover that the wine breaks down those odorous fishy oils. It is the acid in the wine that does it, just as lemon juice or vinegar does; but the wine also adds its delicate perfume.

Wherever you now add water, replace a little of it with wine—and the results will be a more fragrant, better-tasting dish.

Although I offer no recipes here (cookbooks contain thousands, and most beverage stores offer the free recipes produced by the Wine Advisory Board), following are a few general hints about wine in your kitchen.

You normally use three kinds: Sherry, red table wine, and white table wine. They are the same wines you serve as beverages; leftover wines from the dinner table will do. (There is no need to buy special cooking wines; they are only standard wines with salt added—required by some restaurant chefs simply to keep the help from drinking the kitchen supply.)

Sherry doesn't spoil, but red and white table types do once their bottles are opened; so don't keep too much of the latter on hand.

Standard flavor harmonies are white wine for fish and chicken dishes; red wines for red meats; Sherry for shellfish, creamed dishes, and soup. (Concerning the latter, if you don't already know it, the leading canned soups already contain Sherry, part of the secret recipes of the best manufacturers.)

Don't drown foods with wine; a little goes a long way. In fact, your dishes should never actually smell or taste of wine. Mostly what you want is the subtle, elusive, unidentifiable aroma.

When boiling foods, add the wine at the last moment. If a mixture contains wine and cream, better cook it over hot water so it won't curdle.

Meats can be tenderized as well as flavored by soaking in red wine. This is an extra reason to marinate pot roasts, meanwhile adding other flavorings, too.

Sometimes Americans, frightened in their youth by professional "Drys," hesitate to cook with wine for fear of exposing their children to demon alcohol. If you suffer from this fear, relax—because the alcohol, which has a low boiling point, evaporates and passes off completely when heat is applied.

And as for your budget, I know of no other one seasoning as inexpensive, possessing as much magic goodness, as a few spoonfuls of wine.

CHAPTER 13

IS WINE FOR YOU?

IT WOULD BE WELL TO BEGIN this chapter by stating that you should *not* drink wine if: (a) you have a stomach ulcer; (b) you suffer from Bright's disease or any other chronic kidney ailment; (c) you are acutely ill from any cause, or (d) you have religious scruples against the use of any alcoholic beverage.

As for the latter interdiction, it is based on the tragic demonstration furnished during the Volstead era that any form of prohibition leads inevitably to excessive consumption. However, I always get a certain impious satisfaction from the vast volume of alcoholic tonics (including many that have wine as their base) consumed in this country by religious teetotalers, who find the daily use of these nostrums gives them a feeling of well-being.

There is also something weird in the paradox of certain church groups who interpret Scripture as requiring total abstention, while other denominations find, in the same Holy Bible, clear commands to use wine in their most sacred rites of worship. I perceive something grimly comical in the dozens of volumes that have been penned by fanatics in attempts to prove that the recommendations of wine in the Old and New Testaments meant only unfermented grape juice. Anyone who has ever heard of *Saccharomyces ellipsoideus* (wine yeasts) knows that unless the Apostles were familiar with either pasteurization, refrigeration, or sulfur dioxide, the grape juice of the Bible would surely have turned to wine.

The drunkenness common among Moslems, whose religion commands them to abstain from alcohol, is another demonstration that a feeling of guilt produces excesses. In many predominantly Christian countries, including the United States, a kind of mass guilt complex seems to surround the use of alcoholic beverages. But among the Latin nations wine seems specifically excluded from classification with intoxicating liquor. Ask an Italian: "Do you drink?" and he may answer in the negative, because he uses only wine.

Returning to the medical aspects of wine, doctors are now coming to know a good deal about the values of this beverage that they did not know a generation ago. Strangely enough, earlier physicians were aware of the very things that modern science is only now beginning to discover.

Medical history furnishes the explanation of this. For centuries—since the time of Hippocrates, the father of medicine—doctors have observed the beneficial effects of wine upon individuals both in sickness and in health; and its prescription was virtually universal. Then came the modern era of experimental medicine, in which every pharmaceutical substance has had to be tested and to prove its values. Wine, the oldest of remedies, was not among those first subjected to such tests; and as a result, its medical use gradually declined. With the advent of prohibition, the many references to wine in the United States Pharmacopoeia were summarily dropped.

Thus an entire generation of doctors began practicing their profession with virtually no knowledge of the subject.

In more recent years, however, comprehensive programs of wine research have been instituted in many university laboratories and clinics. What Hippocrates and Aesculapius knew is being rediscovered, and some completely new values of wine are being found. In particular, the specialty of geriatrics (treatment of the elderly) is adopting the recommendation of Galen, the ancient Greek physician, who called wine "the nurse of old age." The quotation used in one of my earlier chapters from Dr. Lucia's text, *Wine as Food and Medicine,* lucidly states the modern view of the geriatrist.

It is interesting to note, in this connection, that red Port seems to be the one kind of wine most widely prescribed for the aged.

Today a comprehensive bibliography of medical research aids physicians in selecting wines in the specialties of nutrition, gastroenterology, cardiology, urology, neurology, and psychiatry. Among the most recent findings are new evidence of *dry* wines' value in the treatment of diabetes (with statistical evidence that this disease is rare among regular users); the detection of wine components which act as mild cardiac stimulants; marked effects in reducing basic emotional tension and in protecting against the shocks of sudden stimuli (both of these at very moderate blood-alcohol levels), and somewhat startling values in treating diseases of the digestive tract.

Especially good news to doctors are findings that certain wines are the most effective natural liquid stimulants of appetite for their convalescent patients; that the low sodium content of the beverage permits its inclusion in the unpleasant low-salt diets of patients with heart trouble; and, finally, measured proof of wine's value in promoting euphoria. The latter quality means more rest for complaining patients, and consequently more rest for the doctor.

A number of physicians of my acquaintance nowadays include wine in reducing diets for their obese patients. They cite American and Italian studies showing that wine calories can replace carbohydrate calories and that patients tend to decrease their carbohydrate intake as they increase their wine intake. The internist who once guided me in a sixty-pound weight-losing program allowed me to continue taking my normal half bottle of dry table wine with dinner, and the campaign was successful.

Measurements of typical California wines indicate that red and white table wines contain from 22 to 26 calories per ounce, that Sherry contains 38 to 45, and sweet dessert wines from 45 to 48.

It may be of particular interest to sufferers from gout

that extensive experiments have been conducted recently to determine the effects of various wines upon that most painful form of arthritis. At this writing, however, no evidence has been produced that even excessive quantities of wine, including Port wine, have any measurable effects on gout, either favorable or otherwise.

I have never forgotten the comment of a certain vintner when, some years ago, I showed him the report by Dr. A. L. Soresi of New York that certain wines had been found to have values in the sedation of post-operative cases—when the wines were administered rectally. "For that purpose," my winemaker friend remarked, "I recommend the wine of my principal competitor!"

Researchers exploring the physiological effects of alcohol are now able to tell us with a fair degree of certainty what happens when wine gets past our lips. For example, they confirm the rule, long known to those who must attend cocktail parties for business reasons, that one way to drink and remain sober is first to line our stomachs with a fatty substance, such as cream or olive oil.

Alcohol, when it reaches the stomach and small intestine, passes through the walls of those organs directly into the blood stream. It is the only food you do not digest. But if you have eaten something first, or lined your stomach walls as above mentioned, the absorption will be slower. This is one of the reasons why wine, because its principal use is with meals, is less intoxicating than other beverages.

Once in the blood stream, some of the alcohol is oxidized in the liver and transformed into energy. But a normal-sized drink exceeds the liver's capacity, reaches the heart, and is pumped through the body to attack the fatty nerve tissues—especially those of the brain. What does it do there? It does not stimulate, as has long been imagined. Instead, it is a depressant. Among other things, its action on nerves in the blood vessels causes the vessels to expand. This explains why we get a warm feeling from alcohol: warm blood is entering the small capillaries of the skin. It also explains why some habitual topers develop red noses: those surface blood vessels have been distended so constantly that they remain so.

Almost-pure alcohol—in a highball containing vodka, for example—gets into the blood stream fastest. Wines, however, contain nitrogenous compounds and organic acids, which slow the rate at which their alcohol gets into the blood. Experiments at Yale and Stanford universities have measured blood-alcohol levels when equal concentrations of alcohol in water, wine, beer, and whisky were drunk. They found that from wine, the rate of absorption was markedly slower, and the peak blood-alcohol level reached was lower, than from any of the other beverages. This is another reason why wine is less intoxicating than other drinks, and it suggests that if you really want to get drunk, you should not choose wine.

This raises the question of why there are found, among the drunkards populating the skid roads of some American cities, the miserable human specimen called a "wino" (a word which makes every vintner gag when he hears it).

There even have been police officials who associated the "wino's" assorted sicknesses with the wine he consumes. Medical authorities have had some difficulty in convincing policemen of the rather simple truth: This type of skid-road inhabitant is a chronic alcoholic who cannot afford the price of heavily-taxed liquor. Wine is cheaper—so he gets his alcohol from wine. Studies of the histories of these individuals have shown that they do not even like the taste of wine, that they buy stronger beverages whenever they can afford them, and that most of them began using wine *after* they had become chronic alcoholics.

Medical research has now clearly established that the various diseases to which alcoholics are subject are principally due not to the alcohol they consume but to the proteins and vitamins they don't. They simply are undernourished.

Massive evidence assembled in recent years confirms a further fact—long apparent to anyone who has observed the daily use of wine in France, Italy, and other Latin countries—that the moderate use of this beverage serves as a preventive of alcoholism. Research on this subject has centered in Yale University and in the University of Rome, and is confirmed by extensive studies conducted in Brazil, New York, and California.

There is nothing new in the observation that wine is a temperate beverage; it was known long before Thomas Jefferson wrote: "No nation is drunken where wine is cheap, and none sober where the dearness of wine substitutes ardent spirits as the common beverage." All that is new is the measured scientific proof.

Chronic alcoholism has long been recognized as a disease. It is blamed basically on emotional causes, although some still suspect physical origins as well. Researchers tell us that certain disturbed individuals are compelled to drug themselves to escape facing reality and do so with any form of depressant available—including gasoline, paint thinner, or bay rum if others are unobtainable. Some of them do it with narcotics.

It is the unanimous current scientific view that both the alcoholic and the potential alcoholic (who, some psychiatrists say, can be identified even in childhood) should never drink alcohol in any form—not even wine.

However, quite different matters are the popular American custom of getting drunk on rare occasions like New Year's Eve and college reunions, and the national attitude which makes it seem socially smart to "get high" and even to "pass out." This strange group sense of values, transmitted by adults, including parents, to children of high-school age, is obviously a cause of many community and national problems.

Dr. Karl Bowman, the noted former director of the Langley Porter Psychiatric Clinic, has suggested that these customs exist because they are parts of national or group cultural patterns, and that they are perpetuated with the help of the press and other forms of communication. Dr. Georgio Lolli, of Yale University, supports this view, pointing out that among cultured Italians even a single instance of being drunk in public would cause an individual to be permanently ostracized.

In families where wine is the common beverage, children are usually given wine diluted with water, and drunkenness is looked upon with no less disgust than any other kind of animal misbehavior.

To those who wish merely to drug themselves I cannot recommend wine.

CHAPTER 14

TO THE CONNOISSEUR

THIS CHAPTER IS ADDRESSED TO ALL who fancy themselves as wine connoisseurs, regardless of whether they are actually experts, true connoisseurs, or only wine snobs as defined in my opening chapter.

The members of this small but influential group have a unique opportunity to perform a noble public service. In a nation which drinks relatively little alcohol, in terms of total gallonage—but which takes it in periodic excessive doses—these people can help materially to popularize the civilized beverage, wine.

To encourage temperate, deliberate living in this country, to heighten the popular cultural level and to spread the appreciation of fine food and the contemplative pleasures, would seem rather obviously worth-while. It may even be an urgent necessity. For as the nation's population zooms from the 192,000,000 figure of 1964 toward the 276,000,000 forecast for 1985, the menace of roaming, knife-wielding gangs, inflamed by intoxicants and drugs, seems certain to grow much worse unless some leavening influence is introduced. Besides, there is a gradually spreading sickness for which wine seems to be at least a partial preventive—the national scourge of alcoholism.

This book, of course, is not intended for the minority who comprise the connoisseur group. It is purely an attempt to simplify for the vast majority of Americans a subject still entangled by taboos, by stilted notions of correctness, and by a foggy maze of perplexing labels and general misinformation. To the majority, wine at present seems not worth bothering with.

The result is that this is the last element of luxurious living whose enjoyment is still reserved mainly for the privileged few.

What can the wine-minded minority contribute? Some have already contributed a good deal. Dr. Raoul H. Blanquié, who cut his teeth on corks from France's leading châteaux, is one; he has explained the mysteries of wine to a vast total audience in his many public appearances and by organizing numerous public tastings. Harold H. Price, one of America's greatest experts on the wines of Europe and California, spread the vinous gospel for thirty years. Dr. George A. Selleck, the nation's outstanding non-professional chef, has introduced high cuisine, with the accompaniment of wines, to many thousands at the enormous number of luncheons and dinners for which he prepares menus. Such noted food writers as Jim Beard and Morrison Wood constantly preach a common-sense approach to wine. These are a few; there are many others, of course. They deserve some of the credit for the steady increase in wine use in the United States. (The gains are imposing; the national rate of apparent wine consumption rose from less than two quarts per adult American in 1934 to an all-time high of more than six quarts in 1963.)

But to most of our cognoscenti the idea has never occurred that they, too, can help advance civilized drinking in America. It requires no fervent missionary zeal to take the first step. That is to erase their attitude of condescension toward the wines of this country.

What difference does it make whether the nation drinks foreign rather than American products? It makes this difference: If wine is ever to become a popular beverage in the United States, it will be up to this country's vintners to make it so, by the same mass-production and mass-distribution methods that have installed frozen orange juice and prepared cake mixes in millions of American homes.

The second step is primarily a matter of practical semantics. Our connoisseur cult ought to stop referring to *fine* wines as merely "good" wines—an unfortunate language habit which inevitably implies that all of the popular-priced wines—the wines available to the majority of Americans—are *not* good and are therefore unfit to drink. All the aesthete means, of course, is that he does not consider such wines quite good enough for his own exalted taste. Or perhaps he is merely translating from the French, who call their everyday wines *ordinaires*.

At any rate, it requires no mental magic to reason that

the everyday, standard wines grown here must be accepted by Americans, if wine is to be accepted at all.

Until now most of those who have wine knowledge, or who pretend they have it, have been impeding the cause instead of aiding it. It is one thing for us to like variety in our beverages. It is quite another to ignore entirely, as so many leading Americans do, the excellent vintages of California, New York State, Ohio, and other sections of the country. This is a silent, but eloquent, form of disparagement.

Foreign vintners have often expressed their amazement, upon visiting the United States, to find European wines featured in our restaurants and on the tables of the wealthy. "Why don't you Americans drink the excellent wines produced in your own country?" these visitors ask. In their own homelands, they point out, nobody would even dream of serving any wines but those of the locality.

Can it be that we still feel inferior to Europe? Is this why our choicest menus are still printed in French, without even an English translation of what they mean?

I get a slight case of mental indigestion whenever I read the claptrap in slick magazines, sneering at ". . . the naïve presumption of a little California Pinot Noir," or seriously advocating that every discriminating wine shopper carry in his wallet the ridiculous little laminated card of European vintage years.

Someday someone—as innocent as the little boy in the Hans Christian Andersen fable about the naked emperor in invisible clothes—will exclaim in wonderment and thereby expose the hokum about foreign wines' superiority.

Whatever recognition United States wines have received for their quality thus far has been won in spite of America's elite. This country's vintners have been looked down upon for so long that they themselves fail to realize that they produce some of the finest wines of the world.

They can do better, with a little encouragement. For just as actors and athletes respond to an appreciative audience, winemakers strive most earnestly when their efforts win approval from those who judge them.

I said in an earlier chapter that there is no harm in being a wine snob. The novice can pretend knowledge, enjoy himself, and perhaps eventually learn. But those Americans who are regarded as connoisseurs have a mission to perform. They are the ones who should taste wines instead of labels. They are the people whom the rest of America strives to emulate. By simply furnishing an example, they can help to popularize wine.

INDEX